The Total Woman

Marabel Morgan

The Total Woman

HODDER AND STOUGHTON

LONDON SYDNEY AUCKLAND TORONTO

Scripture quotations identified KJV are from the King James Version
of the Bible.

Scripture quotations identified RSV are from the Revised Standard
Version of the Bible. Copyrighted 1946 and 1952.

Scripture quotations identified PHILLIPS are from *The New Testament in Modern English* translated by J. B. Phillips, 1958. Used
by permission of the Macmillan Company.

Scripture quotations identified LB are from *The Living Bible*. Copyright © 1971 by Tyndale House Publishers, Wheaton, Illinois
60187.

Material from *Managing Your Time* by Ted Engstrom and Alec
Mackenzie. Copyright © 1967 by Zondervan Publishing House.
Used by permission.

TO *my husband Charlie,*
who understands me better than anyone else,
and still loves me.

Contents

PART TWO

MAN ALIVE

PART THREE

SEX 201

PART FOUR

BUILDING BRIDGES

· ·

Acknowledgments

To my dear friend, Anita Bryant, for her encouragement and enthusiasm in making this book a reality;

To Donna Robinson, my "right hand man," friend, ally, and catalyst;

To Dr. Clyde Narramore, whose ideas and teachings in *Psychology for Living* concerning child rearing have changed my way of life;

To Martha Kettler, my inspiration in polishing this manuscript;

To all of the instructors and graduates of the Total Woman classes, of whom I am proud, and to all their husbands who have verified that these principles work!

Part One
The Organization Woman

1 Introduction

I think in superlatives, so naturally I expected that my marriage to Charlie Morgan would be the world's greatest. Both of us were determined to give our best to each other, but my knowledge of what that entailed was nil. I believed in the all-American Cinderella story; marriage was ruffly curtains at the kitchen window, strawberries for breakfast, and lovin' all the time.

Charlie and I had marvelous communication, so things looked very promising. I understood his vibrations; we were on the same wavelength. During the months of our engagement, he studied his law books at my apartment, and in between cases he shared his dreams and fears with me. He told me his lifelong ambitions; he explained what he wanted to accomplish. While telling me of cases he studied all day, he spoke excitedly of torts, contracts, and jurisdiction. I didn't understand most of what he said, but I hung on every word because I loved him. How fortunate

I was to have found such a talkative man. I had heard
about some husbands who never talked with their wives.

I thought that Charlie was a voracious talker. The
night he asked me to marry him, he nearly talked my ear
off before that magic moment. It was my birthday and
we celebrated over a delicious dinner at Miami Beach.
Charlie talked while I ate! Afterward we drove out on the
beach to look at the ocean. What a breathtaking night. A
huge, full moon shone down on the glistening waves.
Stars flashed in the dreamlike atmosphere and I felt like
reaching out to catch one. We sat in the car and watched
that timeless scene as the waves rolled in onshore.

Charlie had a little stack of birthday presents for me.
They were nice and he was sweet, but he wasn't romantic
at all. He just seemed to keep on talking, which was highly
unusual in view of the surroundings. Content, I curled up
in the warmth of his arms and listened, but I was very
drowsy. My full stomach and the hypnotic rhythm of the
waves put me to sleep.

I don't know how long I slept but suddenly Charlie's
words jolted me back to consciousness. ". . . and that's
what I want in a wife," he was saying. My darling, with
his analytical mind, had been outlining the qualities he
wanted in a wife! *What* did he want in a wife? I had
missed it! Was this a proposal?

I responded quickly, however, when he took me eagerly
in his arms and asked, "Will you be that girl?" My drowsi-
ness was gone. Instantly I was wide awake! He reached

. .

in the backseat again, this time for a velvet jewelry box, and placed a gorgeous diamond ring in the palm of my hand.

He was asking me to be his forever. The joy of this moment! Only one nagging thought marred my joy and kept me awake that night. What were all those things he had been saying that he wanted in a wife? I couldn't admit I had slept through it all. I should have been awake. I could have saved myself and Charlie years of misery.

Hey, Remember Me?

In the frantic, two-week break between semesters we were married and we honeymooned gloriously in Florida. The days were sunny, the nights were star-studded. Indeed, married life was strawberries for breakfast and lovin' all the time.

With Florida tans and happy hearts we moved into a three-room apartment. Our meager earthly belongings and limited responsibilities allowed me lots of spare time. I folded Charlie's shirts and spent hours making goodies for him.

As the months passed, however, our lives became more complicated, and we gradually changed. I was amazed to realize that Charlie had stopped talking. He had become distant and preoccupied. Instead of talking heart-to-heart, we never seemed to talk at all. In answer to my questions about his work and the events of the day, I received an indecipherable grunt. Once I grabbed his chin and said, "Hey, remember me? Look me in the eyeball. I'm talking to you!"

One night after a monologue (my own!), I came to the conclusion that Charlie had been the silent type all along —he had forced himself to talk before marriage in order to win me. If I were to have any meaningful conversations, I decided, they would have to be with my girl friends.

Meanwhile, Charlie and I were polite to each other and said things like, "Please pass the salt." We went through the motions of living as though everything was just fine. But it wasn't. I had always thought I could carry on a pleasant conversation with just about anyone, but my husband stunted my confidence.

Have you ever sat across from your husband in a crowded restaurant and wondered, "What on earth can I say to this man I live with, with whom I am intimate?" It baffled me. At dinner one night, everyone in the place was talking enthusiastically and my brain couldn't come up with one intelligent remark to say to the man I loved.

Each evening, when Charlie walked in the front door after work, a cloud of gloom and tension floated in with him. That cloud was almost tangible. His homecoming was supposed to be the high point of my day. I had been waiting all day to love and care for him, but this tension cloud permeated our home atmosphere. We were at each other for some unknown reason. There was a barrier between us.

. .

As the years wore on, things got worse. Those barriers became insurmountable. I didn't know what caused them, and I certainly didn't know how to make them go away. Sometimes they lasted for days, or weeks, or even months. I was helpless and unhappy. I didn't want anything to come between us, especially this nameless, intangible enemy that I could not define or fight.

"I must learn to adjust," I thought. "Thousands have before me." I adjusted. Several years passed. Our little girl Laura arrived, and I poured my life and time into her. Still I pondered my communication breakdown with Charlie and I realized that our tender, romantic times had slowly slipped away, too. We had our moments, but they were few, and I longed for romance.

I thought back to our engagement period. How romantic Charlie had been! He was such a fabulous kisser, but now there were very few kisses. Where was my passionate lover? After a few short years of married life, I found myself sighing as we sat in front of the television set. As the hero on the tube took the heroine in his arms, I yearned for Charlie to take me in his. I wanted him to smother me with kisses, to make my heart pound again in his loving embraces.

All the marriage articles I read explained how changes occurred throughout marriage. Love moves from a high peak of libido during courtship to a more stable, settled kind of love later on. As I looked at my husband, prone in his television chair night after night, I thought, "That's it —we've got settled love." I didn't like it one bit.

. .

Unglued and Uptight

Laura went to daily vacation Bible school when she was four. She came home every day singing a catchy song: "I'm in-right, outright, upright, downright happy all the time." One evening after hearing the song at least nine times, Charlie looked at me in a peculiar way and began to chuckle. "Say," he said, "I have just the song for you. You're 'in-right, outright, upright, downright *uptight* all the time!' "

He laughed and held his sides, but I was crushed. I thought, "Is he kidding or *am* I uptight all the time?" In spite of my sporadic outbursts, I liked to think I was very calm and serene. I thought of myself as a loving wife and mother, who coped beautifully with difficult situations, and who never raised her voice. Of course, it wasn't a true image, but I was not quite ready for my husband's oblique observation.

The next day I cleaned the house vigorously because some friends from the north were coming by. Among other odd jobs, I polished the dining-room table to a high sheen. Charlie came home just before the company arrived and emptied his briefcase—books, keys, loose change, and other odds and ends—guess where? On the dining-room table with the high sheen.

I must admit that I overreacted a little bit. When the mushroom-shaped cloud settled, Charlie looked at me coldly and said with disgust, "Gee, you sure come unglued easily, don't you?"

. .

I stood there, hurt to the core and stunned by his re-mark. "Don't I have a right to react violently? Do I come unglued easily?" I asked myself. "Why am I so uptight? What's happening to me—to us?" I *was* often grouchy. A more accurate description would be "shrewish." When I was, life was no fun. I didn't even enjoy my own company during those times. How could I expect my family to?

I would try harder. I prepared a very nice dinner the next day and determined to be a sweet wife. However, the bottom fell out for me. Over the mashed potatoes, Charlie announced casually that we would be going out the next evening with some business associates. With no malice I blurted out, "Oh no, we can't." And then I began to tell him of the plans I had already made.

A terrible, stony look passed over my husband's face. I braced myself. In icy tones, with obvious control, he asked, "Why do you challenge me on every decision I make?"

"Challenge you?" I repeated. "I don't challenge you."

"I fight and argue with people all day long," he went on, "and I don't intend to come home each night to fight and argue with you."

"Fight?" I protested meekly, "we don't fight."

He said, "From now on when I plan for us to go some-where, I will tell you twenty minutes ahead of time. You'll have time to get ready, and we'll do without all this arguing!"

Well, my beautiful dinner was ruined. I ran upstairs and cried. I felt as if my little world was crumbling all around me. What disturbed me most at the moment was having only twenty minutes to prepare for any event. My own life would be a mystery to me! The finality with which Charlie spoke also scared me. I knew he was serious.

When he didn't come upstairs to comfort me, I had to stop crying. I began to think about our marriage and what exactly was happening. We did love each other. We probably had a better relationship than most couples I knew. But though joined together as husband and wife, we certainly had no unity of spirit.

I knew that those few outbursts didn't mean that divorce was imminent, but I knew too, that we weren't in ecstasy. Taking stock that night in my bedroom, I had to admit to myself that we definitely weren't doing very well. We were not moving forward.

Something drastic had to be done! The proverb "As now, so then" became a distinct possibility for us. Ten years from now, we would hate each other! Being mediocre in any area of life never appealed to me, and least of all, in marriage. I didn't want a marginal marriage; I wanted the best. That night I made a decision to change the collision course I was on.

Charlie the Cheerleader

The change began with my pursuit of knowledge. I bought all the marriage books I could find. I read until I felt cross-eyed at night. I took self-improvement courses.

I studied books on psychology. I studied the Bible. Over and over certain principles emerged and I began to apply them to my marriage—with stunning results.

As I learned to live these principles, my attitudes changed from day to day. Almost immediately, Charlie began to change as well. He began to talk to me in his old way. At times he could hardly get his words out fast enough. I felt like we were dating again. Marriage was fun. The barriers were gone. He began to share his dreams and activities eyeball to eyeball again. One night we sat on the bed and talked to each other for hours about our innermost feelings. I could hardly believe that this soul-to-soul communication had returned.

I noticed that we began to smile at each other. That realization brought a pain to my heart. How far we had drifted apart. How rare a smile had been. During one family fun time over some little incident, I thought with a pang, "Oh wow, it's been such a long time since we've had a good laugh around here."

Instead of Charlie sprawling in his TV chair all evening, we began to cuddle together on the sofa. He patted me as we passed each other in the house. We began acting like teen-agers in love, not like tired, programmed, settled, married folks. It was quite a thrill, I can tell you!

With communication reopened, romance was not far behind. I finally realized that my remote husband had longed for romance as much as I had. One night, after we had been asleep for hours, he woke me. He took me in his arms and said tenderly, "Darling, I just wanted to tell you I love you so very much." Then he rolled right over and promptly went to sleep.

Now maybe your husband wakes you up regularly in the middle of the night to tell you he loves you, but in six years of married life mine never had. I stayed awake for a long time afterward, reliving that moment. I thought, "Can the application of these principles be the cause of this wonderful change in my husband's attitude toward me?"

The next morning at the breakfast table Charlie said to our two little girls, "Everybody who loves Mommy clap their hands!" And they all applauded enthusiastically. This demonstration coming from my staid, proper husband overwhelmed me. My sober lawyer a cheerleader? This was too much!

Later that week, we attended the finals of a tennis match. In the midst of the volleys, my husband kept pulling me close to him. He has always been very reserved in public, not even liking to hold hands. His behavior became so demonstrative that one of our friends remarked, "Say, what's with you two? Are you in love or something?" I wanted to jump up and down and shout, "Yes, and let me tell you how it all came about!"

The changes in my life began to affect Charlie's life patterns in tangible ways. He began bringing me gifts at night. He had never brought gifts home before. It was just something he didn't do. I didn't feel too badly about it. He was just frugal and we both accepted the fact. Even his friends would kid him about a threefold test he applied before buying anything: "Do we need it? Can we afford it? Can we live without it?" Well, by the time he got to number three, almost everything went by the board.

One afternoon he called to find out if I'd be home at three o'clock. I couldn't imagine what was coming and I was stunned to see a truck pull up with a new refrigerator-freezer. I had nagged for a new one for years, and for years he had refused. Every place we lived had an old refrigerator and I wanted one without someone else's germs! My husband had said, "That's ridiculous. This one works. Why buy a new one?" Now, without being nagged, he was beginning to give me what I yearned for.

During my days as a shrew, I had also pleaded with Charlie to let me decorate the family room. For three years I nagged. The decor in that room became a real issue with me. It grated on my personality. I even hated to walk through the room.

Finally, I nagged and insisted so much that Charlie, in desperation, announced, "Look, I *love* the family room exactly the way it is. We are not going to change it and I don't want to hear another word about it—ever." I was especially miserable that night because I knew I had backed him into a corner, and now the issue was closed.

A few months after my decision to change, Charlie said casually at breakfast one morning, "I've been thinking, honey. I guess you can go ahead and do whatever you want in the family room, as far as the decorating goes. And by the way, you might as well do the living room and dining room while you're at it." Well, I stopped squeezing the oranges and started squeezing him!

This brand-new love between us has given us a brand-new life together. The results of applying certain principles to my marriage were so revolutionary that I had to pass them on in the four-lesson Total Woman course, and now in this book. In fact, many of the illustrations used in this book are actual examples taken from Total Woman classes.

For example, one of my friends came to the classes as a last resort. She and her husband were considering divorce, and hadn't spoken a civil word to each other for months. One morning in her kitchen her five-year-old daughter was listening to her parents shout at each other. Finally she said, "When I grow up, I never want to get married. I don't want to act like you and Daddy." The mother was jolted to her senses and knew that she was painting a terrible picture for her little girl.

At the end of the first session, the mother wondered how she could do her assignment, but she was determined to try. When she came to class the second week, she was radiant. "What I've seen this week is unbelievable," she reported. "My husband wasn't even speaking to me when I began, but I did all my assignments. He has never brought me a gift before, but this past week he bought me two nighties, two rose bushes, and a can opener!"

Some of my friends have asked why I want to tell all this. I realize that much of it sounds like something out of a slick magazine, and in a sense it is. The only reason I can share it at all is that my life has changed for the better. If another woman can learn and profit from my mistakes, why not pass it on?

This book is not intended to be the ultimate authority on marriage. Far from it. I don't pretend to have an automatic, ready-to-wear answer for every marriage problem. I do believe it is possible, however, for almost any wife to have her husband absolutely adore her in just a few weeks' time. She can revive romance, reestablish communication, break down barriers, and put sizzle back into her marriage. It really is up to her. She has the power.

If, through reading and applying these principles, you become a Total Woman, with your husband more in love with you than ever before, my efforts in writing this book will have been rewarded.

2 Redeeming the Time

The typical American housewife begins each day with every good intention. As soon as her husband and kids are out the door, she nobly faces the disaster areas. Each one screams, "Clean me." What to do first? The dishes, the beds, the ironing? The groceries, the errands, the car pool? In the midst of all this trauma, the phone rings. This morning it's a friend who is having trouble with her husband. Listening to twenty minutes of a tale of woe colors her own situation. Confronting her own mess, she throws up her hands in despair. The morning is half gone and she thinks, "What's the use?" Depressed, she pours herself another cup of coffee.

She now has several choices for the rest of the day. She may whine, play the martyr, or escape with her box of bonbons to her favorite soap opera. When the kids come home at three o'clock, she screams at them because she's mad at herself.

A doctor's wife stopped by recently to discuss this very problem, which she seems to encounter every afternoon. Her husband diagnosed it as "the 4:30 syndrome." "Each afternoon at approximately 4:30," she said, "I drag myself to the kitchen and think, 'What, oh what, shall I fix for dinner tonight?'" Her symptoms were rather predictable. First, she peeks into the freezer, wishing that her entree could thaw miraculously. Next, she shuffles through the chicken a la king and tuna fish in the cupboard, knowing either of these dishes would rate an "Ugh" from her husband. Frustrated, she gathers the kids into the car, fights the five o'clock traffic to the store, and returns home with a headache and a pound of hamburger. By the time her husband enters the scene, she's had it. She's too tired to be available to him. She blames him for her mundane existence and takes her frustrations out in other activities. At ten o'clock she calls her girl friend and talks for forty-five minutes while her husband sits watching TV. Whenever he makes the first suggestive move toward her, she starts a new project of cleaning or sewing.

Her husband feels lonely and bewildered inside and thinks, "She doesn't want to be with me anymore." Feeling rejected, he acts aloof or grouchy, or sometimes just heads to bed as a protection.

Perhaps you're like many women who say, "I'm sorry, I can't be available. I have seven kids, four car pools, and I'm overworked." I have known bitter and frazzled housewives who have been transformed into calm and gentle

Total Women! By redeeming the time, you too can beat the 4:30 syndrome.

Your $25,000 Plan

When Charles M. Schwab was president of Bethlehem Steel he confronted Ivy Lee, a management consultant, with an unusual challenge: "Show me a way to get more things done," he demanded. "If it works, I'll pay anything within reason."

Lee handed Schwab a piece of paper. "Write down the things you have to do tomorrow," he said. Schwab wrote. "Now number these items in the order of their real importance," Lee continued. Schwab did it. "The first thing tomorrow morning," Lee instructed, "start working on number one and stay with it until it is completed. Next take number two and don't go any further until it is completed. Then proceed to number three, and so on. If you can't complete everything on schedule, don't worry. At least you will have taken care of the most important things before getting distracted by items of lesser consequence.

"The secret is to do this daily," continued Lee. "Evaluate the relative importance of the things you have to get done . . . establish priorities . . . record your plan of action . . . and stick to it. Do this every working day. After you have convinced yourself of the value of this system, have your men try it. Test it as long as you like. Then send me a check for whatever you think the idea is worth."

In a few weeks Charles Schwab sent Ivy Lee a check for twenty-five thousand dollars. Schwab later said that this lesson was the most profitable one he had ever learned in his business career.

If it works for a steel factory, it will work in your house factory. This plan is yours for the taking. Free! You'll have more time, you'll accomplish much more, and you'll be available for your husband.

Culottes and Sneakers

If your husband came home in the next ten minutes, what would he see? Look around right now. Are the cabinet doors open? Are there toys strewn from one end of the house to the other? Are there dirty dishes still in the sink and a vacuum cleaner in the living room? Don't despair. Here's how you can have it looking fit for a king and keep it that way, with precious time left over just for you.

1. *Take a moment* now *and write down everything you have to do tomorrow.* You'll panic if you wait until morning. The day will already be pressing in on you. Don't worry if the list seems endless! You may have a lot of catching up to do.

Just list on one sheet of paper all those little things you must do tomorrow. A friend of mine keeps her notes on separate scraps of paper. Instead of using a master list, she has notes to herself in every room of the house, as well as in the cars. She admitted her daily schedule bounces between chaos and coincidence. Another friend told me, "I keep a list. But I just keep it in my head and save all the time it takes to write things down." From now on, write it down. Let your master sheet do your remembering. You have far more important things to think about.

Include yourself on this list. Write down a time for yourself each day. Include that sewing project, manicure, favorite book, working in the garden, or just taking a nap. Put it on the list or you'll never get to it. Jackie Kennedy kept a list that was maintained hourly when she was First Lady of the White House, and she had a whole battalion of maids and servants. Remember, you're the First Lady of your house, be it white, yellow, large, or small.

2. *Assign a priority to every item on your list.* List these as number one, number two, and so on. When your husband asks you to do something, he expects it to be done without reminding you. The next time he delegates a job to you, write it down. Give it top priority on your list. Many a husband is so convinced that this plan works that now, instead of asking his wife to do anything for him, he just writes it down on her master sheet.

Assign top priority to the unpleasant tasks. I try to face these first things in the morning when I'm fresh, instead of at four o'clock when I've had it. A Total Woman can't function properly with nagging thoughts hovering over her head all day. Move to the top of tomorrow's list those things you tend to keep putting off. Don't sweep your particular weakness under the rug. Face it as a weakness, and tackle it first thing in the morning.

3. *Tomorrow, begin with number one and stick with it until it's accomplished.* Then start on number two and stay with that until it's finished. Go on to number three and finish it. And so on down your list. Complete each job.

What satisfaction there is in doing one job thoroughly and not having to return to it! Early in the day, as you see items checked off, you'll begin to feel a sense of accomplishment in all that you've done already. I love to scratch off each item as I finish it; I feel encouraged to march right down that list.

Don't worry if you can't complete everything on your list; the most important items will have been done. There's no other way you could have accomplished more, and just look at what you did.

4. *Keep your daily schedules in a loose-leaf notebook, or use a calendar with spaces large enough to enter your daily activities.* This way you keep a running log of your activities. You'll also have a ready record of when you mailed that package, when John's suit went to the cleaners, or when you called the repairman.

Driving to the store one night, Margaret noticed a host of cars in the parking lot of her church. She wondered what was happening, when suddenly, midway between the church and the supermarket, she remembered. Tonight was her committee meeting and she was in charge! Because she was twenty minutes late already, she raced back to the church and conducted the meeting in her culottes and sneakers.

The next day she told the Total Woman class about her calamity. Instead of using her master sheet, she had taped a note to herself on the hood of the stove, and then left the house through the front door!

ABC Business

At the top of my daily $25,000 plan I put, "Prepare dinner after breakfast." When I first tried it, I must admit that the thought of it rather nauseated me. I had always tried to get out of the kitchen as quickly as possible. But I found that I could still make this goal and have an edge on dinner besides.

How? First I decide my evening menu the day before and write it at the top of the list. Each morning I make the salad or dessert or set out the ingredients for dinner. Many a Total Woman sets the table for her already completed dinner at 9:00 A.M. and never worries about the 4:30 syndrome. You can too, if you set your mind to it. You can have all your home duties finished before noon. You can have a place for everything and everything in its place.

I am an incurable optimist, but being married to a lawyer, I have learned to anticipate every possible problem that might arise in a given situation. I sometimes think, "Whatever can go wrong, probably will!" That brings me back to earth. Therefore, I'm ready with an alternate plan. If things go well, fine. I am most surprised and pleased. If not, I'll put Plan B into effect.

So often, unexpected events come my way that aren't on my $25,000 plan. Children get sick, friends drop by, and my washing machine breaks down. Who knows? My husband sometimes calls and asks me out for lunch! Knowing full well that life is full of changes, I try not to panic when a monkey wrench is thrown into my day. I try to stay calm by putting into practice Plan B (or C or D, depending on how many curves I am thrown that day). I am learning to welcome interruptions.

A neighbor trudged into my house the other day looking like a tired Phyllis Diller. She was laughing, not crying, when she said, "Well, I'm down to Plan G now, but would you believe, I haven't lost my cool yet? It's amazing how differently I see problems now. It's almost a challenge to see if I can make Plan B work as well as my original plan. This ABC business is like a game I play with the fates of the day, and I'm winning!" Here was a happy and flexible Total Woman.

Learn to capitalize on disappointment and heartbreak. That's not heartless, that's wise. Make things that go wrong part of your plan. Adversity can make you better instead of bitter. In the Bible, James says, "When all kinds of trials and temptations crowd into your lives, my brothers, don't resent them as intruders, but welcome them as friends" (1).

God allows heartbreak so man will learn to trust Him. King Solomon, the world's wisest man, knew this well. He developed a marvelous habit to prevent heartache. Each day he prayed over his master list, "Commit thy works unto the LORD, and thy thoughts shall be established" (2). I'm beginning to pray over my list. Instead of spinning my wheels, I need success. This practice gives an exciting new dimension to life.

Those who try this $25,000 plan swear by it. It has changed many lives. If you put it to work for yourself, whatever your nature, you'll be more organized and efficient. You will accomplish more with less effort than you ever thought possible. With your dinner prepared, you can soak in a five o'clock bubble bath, which will be part of your plan. You will have energy to spare, and a sense of accomplishment that is necessary for happy living.

As for your husband, he will be thrilled. Every man appreciates order and he'll be especially glad to find it in his own home. He will be pleased with you, your accomplishments, and your sense of well-being. When you're organized and efficient, his flame of love will begin to flicker and burn.

Tomorrow is a new day. Wake up to your $25,000 plan.

3 Interior Decorating

Jim and Donna Robinson were returning from the mountains with their little girls. For two weeks Donna's two-year-old had "walked" the distance on her mother's knees, and Donna had reacted accordingly. She was extremely frustrated by her lack of rest and relaxation. The whole vacation had been such a waste.

To ease the tension among all of them, Jim stopped for lunch in a small, quaint town. Before lunch they took a walk through the park and adjoining cemetery. It was the quietest they'd been the entire trip. Walking through the rows of tombstones, Donna absentmindedly read the epitaphs and came upon the grave of a mother. The inscription read: SHE WAS THE SUNSHINE OF OUR HOME.

During lunch Donna kept thinking to herself, "If I dropped over right here, that would probably be the last thing they'd put on my tombstone." So from that point on she decided she would do everything in her power to be the sunshine in her home and the remainder of the vacation became 100 percent more pleasant.

You have the power to lift your family spirit or bring it down to rock bottom. The atmosphere in your home is set by you. If you're cheery tonight, chances are your husband and children will also be cheery. If you're a crab, they probably will be too, since they take their cues for daily living from you.

How is your attitude toward your daily duties? Are you pleasant to live with, even when your husband doesn't appreciate your efforts? Do you know that your personal happiness depends on the attitude you decide you will have? It does. Norman Vincent Peale said that attitudes are more important than facts. You can decide now on what level you are going to live, regardless of your husband's attitudes.

One husband said, "I'm tired of paying all these shopping bills. Will you stop spending so much money!" His wife's favorite store was having a sale, so she thought he was being deliberately mean. She allowed her attitude to register a negative response. She clammed up for days. She had no desire to do anything around the house. The dirty clothes piled up and could have blown away as far as she was concerned. She was wiped out emotionally and physically, because her attitude controlled her behavior.

A great marriage is not so much finding the right person as *being* the right person. Most of the women I know would like to improve their roles as wife and mother, which are primarily concerned with things they *do*. Their role as a woman is something they *are*, and that gets us down to basics.

One girl in class winced and said, "I've got a lot of interior decorating to do. Looks like I'll be busy for a while." She was right. Interior decorating on your attitudes does take a little work, but the results that come your way are more than worth the effort.

Winning Game Plan

You can become the sunshine in your home, but first you must learn where the clouds are. It was Socrates who said, "To know yourself is the beginning of wisdom." Jesus promised, "Ye shall know the truth, and the truth shall make you free" (3). It's easy to say, but how does one go about understanding herself?

As an opener, I find that it helps to write out your philosophy of life as a woman. This takes some time and thought on your part, but it is most beneficial to have in writing your basic feelings about life.

As a guideline, you can ask yourself, Who am I? Where am I going? Why am I here? Taking the time to consider these questions often brings the answers. One girl panicked at this suggestion because she had no philosophy of life. Later she commented, "This class assignment was the greatest challenge of my life. Writing out my ideas forced me to evaluate exactly where I was heading." Now she knows.

If you know anything about the game of football (the game that mesmerizes your husband week-in and week-out), you know that each team has a game plan. The coach with the winningest team has the best-laid plans. Do you have a plan for your game of life? There is something about a woman who knows where she's going in life that makes her a very interesting partner. How do you become that kind of woman?

The Possible Dream

Take a good look at yourself, "Coach." Begin by making a list with four columns: strengths, weaknesses, short-term goals, and long-term goals.

1. *List your areas of strength.* There is great potential within you, undeveloped resources that you've not begun to tap. Take a look at what you do well. What's your favorite pastime? Do your homemaking talents bring you satisfaction? Does your cooking bring raves? Do you make people feel good? Do you have special ability or education that contributes to society? Use these hidden talents. Develop them. You can be better than you even thought you were!

2. *What are your weaknesses?* Honestly list every area where you feel insecure. You will need to consider your weaknesses in the light of your childhood. It may have been happy or tragic, or a bit of both. Naturally, those years had a tremendous effect on how you react to life today. You brought those reaction patterns to your marriage. Whatever your background, problems within you

can only be worked out today. That's encouraging because you have today.

Write down your most embarrassing moment, your hurts, your fears. Recall your moments of success and see how they helped build some of your strengths today. Writing down your past helps you understand yourself.

You need not show anyone what you've written. This is you, exposed and open. You don't have to play a role now. Why did you act as you did? Why did your family progress as it did? Consider the strengths and weaknesses of your parents. What did you love about your mother? your father? What did you dislike about them? In times of stress, how did you comfort yourself? Did you cry, or eat, or spend money?

Take time now to do this. Write down your thoughts. It's marvelous therapy and well worth the effort. Resentment within you is like a splinter in your foot. It hurts deep down, unconsciously perhaps, but it hurts. When you pull the splinter, when you name the problem and face it, the sore can heal.

This exercise may not eradicate any of your weaknesses, but it may help you build those weaknesses into strengths. The coach who has only a puny right tackle must play him, but the other players will compensate for him and the puny tackle will give 110 percent.

3. *Write down your short-term personal goals—not the goals you have set for your husband, but yours.* List the things you are working toward as an individual, as a wife, and as a mother.

Try it. Stop reading right now and write down your

present goals. Then break them into columns for tomorrow, this week, and this month. List everything that's on your mind. Don't try to be too profound. Some of your most basic goals may seem so simple. A salesman's wife told me that her short-term goals were to run a smooth home, cook good meals, be a listening mother, be more fun and less frumpy. The next morning she started the day with such a difference in her attitude. She felt worthwhile because she was working toward her goals.

Another girl listed as her goals: invite the boss to dinner, clean out the closets, exercise, quit smoking, get caught up on correspondence, and lose weight. In assigning priorities, losing weight became number one. She lost fifteen pounds in six weeks. Her husband loved her new body so much that he bought her a whole new wardrobe. You've never seen a happier woman.

Your short-term list will also serve as a sifting device for those things that don't require immediate attention. Things like cleaning the linen closet or polishing the silver may be transferred to your $25,000 plan for tomorrow or may be postponed for two weeks.

4. *List your long-term goals.* In ten years, what do you hope to be? Be specific. List the areas in your life that you would like to improve as a wife and mother. You can attain your goals; your dream is not impossible.

Uglies and All

A young woman wrote in her philosophy for class, "I believe my husband loves me, which is a blessing; I'm not too sure if I love him. I love God and my children. Maybe it's myself I don't love. I seem to be in a never-never land and certainly would love to be more alive in the right-now-and-here land."

Many American women today have never accepted themselves. "If only I were beautiful," so many dream. "If only I had more money, if only I had married someone else, if only, if only." What a tragic way to live. Very few women are married to millionaires. Very few women look like beauty queens. And even if they did, that wouldn't necessarily satisfy. Recently, a former Miss America revealed she had the "uglies," and couldn't stand to look at herself in the mirror.

Jesus said, ". . . Thou shalt love thy neighbour as thyself" (4). If you do not love yourself, you are incapable of loving others, for you have nothing to give. Furthermore, if you don't love yourself, your husband can't fully love you either.

Centuries ago, David wrote in the Psalms, "I will praise thee; for I am fearfully and wonderfully made" (5). If you can change yourself, do it. If you can't, accept yourself as God's creation—who, what, and why you are.

After your bath tonight, stand before the mirror and look at your body carefully. Say to that girl in the mirror, "I accept me as I am, bulges, hang-ups, and all." It may not be as easy as it sounds, but it's so important. Face each weakness, and realistically accept the fact that it exists. You're only human. You, as well as everybody else, have your limitations, so welcome aboard. Don't be too hard on yourself; don't put yourself down.

A friend once told me, "It's almost as if I needed permission to love myself." Perhaps it sounds self-centered to love yourself, but it's most necessary if you're going to love others, including your husband. When you do, you will have a good image of yourself. That means you like being you. You will function properly and accomplish what you set out to do. You will have a sense of well-being within.

When you understand, accept, and love yourself, you are then free to *be* yourself. Shakespeare said:

> This above all: to thine own self be true
> And it must follow, as the night the day,
> Thou canst not then be false to any man.

He was so right, even four hundred years ago! Be true to yourself and be yourself. You are a great person to be!

Poise and self-confidence are available to any woman. Discover who you really are and where you are going. Develop your own convictions. Have the courage to live by your standards. Enjoy your unique spot in the world.

Understanding, acceptance, and love are processes. They may not happen in a day, a week, or a year. But as you begin, you are on your way. You are preparing yourself to reach out to your husband, your children, your friends, and the world. You need not be an onlooker. You can jump right into the middle of life once you are secure within yourself. You will no longer watch things happen or ask, "What happened?" *You* will be what's happening.

Assignment

1. Make a list of everything you must accomplish tomorrow. Assign each a priority and then tackle that $25,000 plan!

2. Write out your own philosophy of life. Ask yourself, "Who am I, where am I going, and why?"

3. Make a list of all your strengths and a list of all your weaknesses. Be realistic and honest. Then, by an act of your will, accept your weaknesses. Determine to maximize your strengths by taking specific action.

4. Set a goal, one specific goal, to be reached one week from today. List everything you will need to accomplish this goal. Incorporate this list into your master plan for the week to come.

5. Set one long-term goal and determine to make it yours.

THE ORGANIZATION WOMAN

Part Two
Man Alive

4 Accept Him

Sandy and Tom are newlyweds. I've known them both since their engagement and have watched their marital ups and downs. Sandy took the Total Woman class recently and wrote to me several weeks later to tell about her results.

"Two years ago," she began, "I walked down the aisle to say 'I do,' but inside I was already thinking how to redo. I began to work him over, subtly at first and then head-on. That's where my problems began. Now I've stopped nagging him and started accepting him as he is. He's a new man and we're a new couple. Thanks a million for the class!"

It's true that most of us marry a man with every intention of changing him. Then we spend years of married life trying to do just that—round off the edges, suggest what he should do, and how he should act. Why are we such fools? It never works! The poor husband crawls into his shell to protect himself from the onslaught, vowing never to communicate with this relentless woman who was once his bride.

A man needs to be accepted as he is, just exactly as he is. This kind of all-out acceptance convinces him you really love him. His need for total acceptance isn't so strange; I need to feel accepted too. Don't you? Doesn't everyone?

Do you have a special friend who will listen to your innermost heart and accept you, no matter what? I do. We can sit in the backyard or talk on the phone, and I feel free to unburden my heart to her. I can be myself without any fear of rejection, criticism, or advice. She won't put me down or laugh at me. I'm free to be me without playing games. She just listens and loves me as I am. I love her because she loves me.

Can you do less for your husband? Can't you accept him as you would a good friend? Your husband needs your acceptance to free him the same way. If so, there won't be enough hours for him to spend with you. The barriers between you will just melt away.

My Husband, My Friend

Unfortunately, I'm a nag by nature. I don't mean to be; it just works out that way. Nagging is my occupational hazard. All day long I direct my kids: "Pick up your clothes, brush your teeth, and don't get out of bed." When my husband walks in the door, I just naturally continue my commands: "Take out the garbage, be kind to my mother, smile at people," and on and on.

For six years I nagged Charlie on the same subjects day after day. Finally, he couldn't take it any longer. He told me firmly one night, "Stop your nagging! I heard you the first time. I'm not your child; I'm your husband."

I was a bit stricken at first, but I couldn't get those words out of my head. I felt powerless. How in the world would the garbage ever get taken out if I couldn't remind him hourly? After all, I was only trying to be helpful!

I thought back over the previous week and replayed in slow motion some of the more dominant scenes. I noticed that Charlie's reactions had fallen into a pattern. If I nagged him continually, he simply tuned me out; he had heard me the first time. If he didn't clam up, as he usually did, he'd blow his cork.

"You're always telling me to take out the garbage," he exploded one night. "You've told me four times tonight to take it out. You know it always gets taken out. But I deliberately refuse to take it out until you quit bugging me about it!" Backed into a verbal corner, he was fighting for the right to be himself. He chose the exact opposite of what I wanted, to prove he was the leader!

I was also beginning to sound like his second mother, according to psychiatrists, and there was no way he could feel romantic toward his second mother. I saw that if I continued to nag, I would only polarize our positions. I also realized that the usual reactions on his part might lead to resentment and/or retreat to the golf course, the office, or even another woman.

One thing I knew for sure. My nagging wasn't bringing results. I determined that night not to nag Charlie again about the garbage. I wouldn't say a word, even if it piled up for weeks. But to my surprise, gals, he took out the garbage the very first night—completely without my assistance. Remarkable!

Then I decided to stop nagging altogether. I would bite my tongue instead. I would say it once and then the decision was his. I finally realized that my man's home is his castle, or at least it should be. He should feel free in the privacy of his own castle, free to do what he wants, even if that means draping his clothes on the furniture, drawing pictures on the walls, or eating pizza for forty-seven straight days. Nagging him over trivia will only drive him up the wall or out the door.

A housewife wrote to marriage columnist Ann Landers, asking her to encourage wives to nag their husbands for their health's sake. "The wife," the letter said, "should nag if he eats too much, drinks too much, smokes too much, if he doesn't exercise enough," and so on. She ended the letter with the plea, "Please tell women everywhere who love their husbands to nag them. It could add years to their lives."

Ann's reply was pure genius. "Who wants more years like that? Sorry, I don't agree. Nagging never kept anyone alive. It has, however, killed many marriages. A man considers being nagged at worse than being nibbled to death by a duck."

If you have an emotional need to nibble, it's much safer to call a girl friend as your sounding board. Call a buddy who will keep your confidence and won't take your nagging to heart. Release your steam on her instead of on your tired husband. A nag or critic doesn't make for a long marriage or a healthy husband.

Nagging is the opposite of accepting. If you have the habit, you know it's a hard one to kick. Nip it in the bud by admitting verbally what you're doing. You'll find that once you accept your husband, you'll no longer need to nag. Just that thought alone may send him into ecstasy!

One wife who kicked the habit after eighteen years reported, "The most amazing thing has happened. His faults really don't bother me. They're not my concern now. I just concentrate on his good points and I love him so much more than I ever did before."

Salad, Sex, and Sports

Your husband is what he is. Accept him as that. This principle is as old as life itself. God accepts us as we are. Even though we don't deserve it, He still loves us. He has no angle. His love is unconditional. Because He accepts us, through His power we can love and accept others, including our husbands.

One woman balked at this idea. "I don't even love my husband anymore, let alone accept him," she said. "He doesn't deserve to be accepted." This seems to be the case in so many homes. What's the cure for this marital malady?

First of all, the Bible says that wives should love their husbands. If you've lost the love for your husband, why not ask God to restore it? Secondly, if you want your marriage to succeed, you must choose to accept him, knowing that your relationship will probably not improve if you don't. The choice is yours—you can choose to either go on living with resentment or accept your husband.

If you choose the latter course, how do you start? Simply make up your mind to accept him just as he is. By an act of your will, determine that you won't try to change him no matter what. That's supreme love.

The change I saw in one couple was remarkable. The wife had thought long and hard before making this decision. But once she did, her husband spotted the difference immediately. "*He* has changed so much," she told me. "He's so much more loving and generous. He wants to give me money all the time! I'm going to start taking it just to make him happy!"

Some women don't nag verbally, but their nonaccepting vibrations communicate loud and clear. With heaving sighs over the kitchen sink, the martyr silently nurses her woes. "I do accept my husband," she thinks. "I've been putting up with his faults for years without saying a word, but he'll never change. I won't say anything. I'll just carry on for the sake of the children."

Tolerance is not acceptance. Your tolerance only makes your husband feel incomplete and unworthy. He can sense when he's not being accepted, and is not able to love you fully.

Your husband needs your acceptance most of all during his times of apparent failure. If he's already low, don't put him down further. Never compare him with another man. And remember, he'll never confide in you if he feels that you are being critical or are trying to change him.

Life is too short to dwell on another's weaknesses. Concentrate on his strengths.

Your man needs to feel important, loved, and accepted. If you won't accept his idiosyncrasies, who will? A Total Woman caters to her man's special quirks, whether it be in salads, sex, or sports. She makes his home his haven, a place to which he can run. She allows him that priceless luxury of unqualified acceptance.

The Man, not the Plan

Having lived on both sides of the fence, I can tell you where the greener pastures are. During my early years of married life, I led a one-woman crusade to make my man into my mold. One particular irritation was that Charlie was constantly on the phone with his stockbroker. A dozen times a day they conspired, and each time I became more and more upset. First of all, I was jealous of the time Charlie spent on the phone. Secondly, I was worried sick that he'd gamble away all our savings.

One day the broker, who also happened to be a family friend, called me on the phone. He knew that Charlie was at work and he gave me some advice: "Let your husband do what he wants in the market. Don't ever tell him what to do with his money. You stay out of it and take care of the kitchen."

Oh, boy, did that burn me up! I was furious at both of them! But the wise, old gentleman had sensed my animosity. He had seen that I wasn't accepting Charlie's role as provider, nor was I submitting to his family leadership.

Today my attitudes have changed, and we're both much happier because of it. I have determined to support my husband's plan, and if that seems impossible, at least I'll support the *man!*

If you too make this decision, be sincere. Your husband may be surprised by your change of attitude, and react with suspicion. His love cannot be aroused by something contrived by a manipulative wife.

One wife said accusingly to her husband, "I've made radical changes around here for two whole weeks, and you haven't changed at all." He replied, "You've made two-week changes before; I'm waiting to see if it's permanent." His coals of love had been dormant for so many years that it took more than a spark to relight his fire. Her attempted manipulation fizzled; he had been burned before.

Once you begin accepting your husband, you can stop worrying about your role as his chief advisor. He doesn't need your advice; he needs your acceptance. Tremendous pressure will be lifted from you, not to mention the pressure lifted from him! He will probably begin to reveal his thoughts to you, and he may even choose to do exactly what you've been wanting!

Accepting your husband is the first step in making your man come alive, and it works. It frees him to become a Total Man. He has that potential, but is unable to attain it until you allow him to be himself. Accept him, just as he is today. Accept his strengths and weaknesses, ". . . for better for worse, for richer for poorer, in sickness and in health . . . from this day forward."

5 *Admire Him*

Psychiatrists tell us that a man's most basic needs, outside of warm sexual love, are approval and admiration. Women need to be loved; men need to be admired. We women would do well to remember this one important difference between us and the other half.

Just the other day a woman told me, "My husband doesn't fulfill me. He never tells me his real feelings; he never expresses his love. He's about as warm as a cold fish!"

Your man, like so many American males, may be like an empty cup emotionally. He may seem void of emotions, unable to properly express his real feelings to you. Why is this? Remember that he grew up in a culture that taught him not to cry when he scratched his leg. Instead of hugging Uncle Jack, he shook hands. Grown-ups were generally unavailable to listen, so he learned to keep his feelings to himself.

We girls, on the other hand, were allowed to cry and

throw temper tantrums. We were encouraged to kiss baby dolls, Aunt Susie, and the baby-sitter. We grew up full of emotions and knew basically how to express love. Then one day the fun began. Mr. Cool married Miss Passion. Is it any wonder that she felt unfulfilled because he never showed her any emotion?

Have you ever wondered why your husband doesn't just melt when you tell him how much you love him? But try saying, "I admire you," and see what happens. If you want to free him to express his thoughts and emotions, begin by filling up his empty cup with admiration. He must be filled first, for he has nothing to give until this need is met. And when his cup runs over, guess who lives in the overflow? Why, the very one who has been filling up the cup—you!

Love your husband and hold him in reverence, it says in the Bible. That means admire him. *Reverence*, according to the dictionary, means "To respect, honor, esteem, adore, praise, enjoy, and admire."

As a woman, you yearn to be loved by that man, right? He, being a man, yearns to be admired by you. And he needs it first. This irritates some women until they see that they have certain strengths that a man doesn't have. It's a great strength, not a weakness, to give for the sheer sake of giving. It is your nature to give. Calvin Coolidge once said, "No person was ever honored for what he received. Honor has been the reward for what he gave."

You are the one person your husband needs to make him feel special. He married you because he thought you were the most enchanting girl of all. The world may bestow awards on him, but above all others, he needs your admiration. He needs it to live. Without it his motivation is gone.

A young executive was literally starved for admiration from his wife. She wanted him to fulfill her before she met his needs. She explained, "Why should I give in first? Marriage is a fifty-fifty deal. I'm not about to give everything." Her husband threw himself into his business, working extra-long hours. He hoped his work would fill up that inner emptiness.

During a Total Woman class, this wife realized that she had the power to pour into him the admiration he needed. She began to admire him. Their relationship began to change. One evening he told her, "Something beautiful is happening. I don't know what it is, but it's great. You seem more alive for some reason."

Hero Worship

Try this test for a week. Starting tonight determine that you will admire your husband. By an act of your will, determine to fill up his cup, which may be bone dry. Be positive. Remember that compliments will encourage him to talk.

Admire him as he talks to you. Concentrate on what he's saying. Let him know you care. Put your magazine down and look at him. Even if you don't care who won yesterday's football game, your attention is important to him and he needs you. Let him know he's your hero.

Don't interrupt or be preoccupied. A pilot told me, "When my wife is indifferent and doesn't respond to what I'm saying, it shatters me for two or three days. Indifference is the worst pain of all."

Another woman called me the night she was sued for divorce. When she asked her husband why, she was shocked at his reply: "You've always been completely indifferent to my life. You never cared what I did or thought."

Every marriage needs tact—that special ability to describe another person as he sees himself. Your husband needs you to see him as he sees himself. For example, take a good look at him. He happens to love his body. It's the only one he has and he lives in there. He wants you to love it too. The only way he'll ever know that you do is for you to tell him.

Perhaps this sounds very foreign to you. You may even think it vulgar. If so, your husband is probably long overdue for some badly needed praise. It is your highest privilege to assure him that he is as special as he hoped he was.

Tonight when he comes home, concentrate on his body. Look at him, really observe him. It may have been years since you actually looked at him with eyes that see. Try looking at him through another woman's eyes—his secretary's or your neighbor's. That might help bring him into focus.

Tell him you love his body. If you choke on that phrase, practice until it comes out naturally. If you haven't admired him lately, he's probably starving emotionally. He can't take too much at once, so start slowly. Give him one good compliment a day and watch him blossom right before your eyes.

Look for his admirable qualities. Even the ugliest man has certain qualities worth admiring, but we're talking about the dream man you married. Compliment that one who used to make your heart pound and make your lips stammer. Admire that one who stood far above the crowd of common men.

Pick out his most masculine characteristics and let him know they please you. His whiskers, for instance. The day he shaved for the first time was a milestone in his life. But have you ever complained with irritation, "Ouch, why don't you shave once in awhile? You're rubbing my face raw"? You can compliment your husband into shaving off his weekend whiskers by reinforcing his masculine image. Tell him nicely, "Honey, your scratchy beard is too strong for my tender skin."

Thin Arms, Full Heart

Admire him *personally*. This is what he is yearning for. When he comes home tonight would you rather have him admire your newly waxed floor, or tell you how great you look? In the same way, he'd rather hear how handsome he is, than how great his corporation is.

Tomorrow morning watch your husband when he looks in the mirror. He sees an eighteen-year-old youth, with firm stomach muscles and a full head of hair. No matter what his age, he doesn't see his pouch or receding hairline. He sees what he wants to see, and wants you to see that eighteen-year-old, too. Of course, this isn't really so strange. What age girl do you see in the mirror? My own grandmother admitted to feeling that she was not much past twenty-one.

A dentist's wife told me she had blurted out one night, "Look, you're getting fat and bald. It's disgusting. Why don't you just face the truth? You're not a kid anymore." The first shot had been fired. Her husband felt devastated and to protect himself, he lashed out at her weaknesses in a brutal way that only he could do. He could not rationally answer her comment but instead struck out at her personally.

In class one day, I gave the assignment for the girls to admire their husband's body that night. One girl went right to work on her homework. Her husband was shorter than she, but quite handsome. In all their years together she had never put her admiration into words. It was a big step for her. She didn't quite know how to start, even though it was her own husband. That evening while he was reading the paper, she sat down next to him on the sofa and began stroking his arm. After a bit, she stopped at the bicep and squeezed. He unconsciously flexed his muscle and she said, "Oh, I never knew you were so muscular!" He put down the paper, looked at her, and inquired, "What else?" He was so starved for admiration, he wanted to hear more!

The next day, she told this to her girl friend, who also decided to try it. Her husband had thin arms, but she admired his muscles anyway. Two nights later she couldn't find him at dinner time. He was out lifting his new set of weights in the garage! He wanted to build more muscles for her to admire.

By the way, admiration can also work wonders for your children. For example, one mother always nagged her son to hop out of the car to open the garage door. One afternoon she said, "Tommy, I'll bet a boy with muscles like yours could flip that garage door up in nothing flat." That's all she said, and that's all he needed. She never again had to ask him to open the door.

Your husband won't mind helping you either, if he's approached in the proper way. Instead of struggling with a jar and breaking a fingernail, ask him to loan you his strong hands for a minute. He derives pleasure from showing off his strength, even on a little old jar.

I know of only one case where this principle backfired. One wife asked her husband, one of the Miami Dolphin football players, to give her a muscular hand with the jars. Finally he asked, "Say, what's with you? You've been opening these baby food jars for five months and now all of a sudden you can't seem to manage them." So don't overdo it. Give him only the jars you really can't handle.

Rebuilding a Partial Man

I heard one wife say, "I feel guilty using feminine wiles on my husband. It seems dishonest. Anyway, his ego is so big, it doesn't need expanding. His body is not all that great. Why should I lie to build him up? I want to be honest, but still meet his needs."

If you're secure within yourself, you won't be afraid to give your husband credit. Instead of feeling threatened, you will feel joy in meeting his needs. As you know, you cannot express love to your husband until you really love yourself. But once you do, you can give with abandon. In fact, you can give with no thought of what you'll receive in return.

I am not advocating that you lie to give your husband a superficial ego boost; even a fool will see through flattery. But I am saying he has a deep need for sincere admiration. Look for new parts to compliment as you see him with new eyes

Consider his weaknesses and things about which he may be self-conscious. Larry had a nasty scar on his neck as the result of an accident. His wife knew that it upset him and saw that he kept rubbing it. She said, "I really love your scar, honey. It makes you look so rugged." Her admiration made him feel relieved inside and less self-conscious.

If you haven't been communicating much lately with your husband, you may have trouble finding something to compliment. If that's your case, think back to those days when you were first convinced that he was the one. What did you love about him then?

An older couple was so estranged that the wife could not see anything to admire about her husband. She forced herself to think back, all the way to the Depression days, when he frugally kept the family together with shrewd business management. Now, nearly forty years later, she shyly mentioned how she had admired his financial leadership during that time. Those were the first appreciative words he had heard in years, and his reaction was pitiful. He looked at her with disbelieving eyes, tears welled up, and though he found no way of verbally expressing his appreciation, he was very tender that evening. The wife was amazed that such a little remark from the distant past could cause this behavior. It was a turning point in their marriage.

A marriage must not remain stagnant. You can keep yours exciting and growing, and in order to succeed, you must. At the end of a long day, your husband especially needs your compliments. One husband called his wife just before quitting time to say, "This is a partial man looking for a Total Woman; be prepared!"

Put your husband's tattered ego back together again at the end of each day. That's not using feminine wiles; that is the very nature of love. If you fulfill his needs, he won't have to escape some other way.

On the other hand, you may have a husband who does not do anything but stay home drinking beer in his underwear. The responsibility of the family may rest on your back because somewhere along the line you usurped his role. Your nagging may have taken the wind out of his sails and now he has no desire to keep working for you.

Your husband may need your compliments to restart his engine, regardless of the distance or bitterness between you. Life is made up of seemingly inconsequential things, but often it's a little thing that can turn the tide. Behind every great man is a great woman, loving him and meeting his needs. There are some exceptions to this, but very few.

Self cries, "Love me, meet my needs." Love says, "Allow me to meet your needs." Dish out some sincere compliments to your man tonight, and watch his cup fill up and overflow. What nagging cannot do, admiration will!

6 *Adapt to Him*

One Monday morning Bobbie Evans, the wife of Miami Dolphins tackle Norm Evans, arrived at my doorstep fed up and resentful. The football team was flying in at noon and she was picking up Norm at the airport. Bobbie needed to talk out her anger to a buddy before she unloaded it on her husband. She was tired of Norm's never-ending football schedule, his endless appearances and speaking engagements, and her having to bear sole responsibility for disciplining the children. In fact, the heartbreaking question of her little boy, "Isn't Daddy ever coming home for dinner again?" prompted her to seek a solution.

She felt lonely, neglected, and unloved. The situation didn't look good. I wondered what to tell her—put her foot down? insist that he quit football? demand that he spend more time at home? threaten him? She had already tried that for two years, but of course nothing had changed. Should I tell her to withhold her love? make

him come begging to her? play the martyr? She had tried
that too. Result? No change.

What I told her, she didn't like. Later she admitted, "I
was so mad, I almost got up and walked out. I certainly
hadn't come over to hear that *I* should adapt to *Norm's*
life."

Adapting was the only thing I knew that would work.
"Bobbie," I told her, "adapt to his way of life whole-
heartedly, even if he doesn't come home for weeks. When
he is home, make life so attractive he won't want to
leave. Don't make him feel guilty and don't complain.
Instead, treat him like a king and cater to his needs."

Bobbie cried a little, but finally dried her eyes and
smiled. "I'm going to do it," she said. The first thing Norm
said when he got off the plane and saw her radiant face
was, "Hey, what's happened to you?" Nothing had
changed except Bobbie's attitude. The unreal schedule
was still the same, but Bobbie had determined to adapt.

Two years later, Norm told her one night during sweet
communion, "I love you so much right now that if you
asked me to quit playing football, I'd do it." She wouldn't
ask him to; she has adapted to his way of life. By the
way, he has become an All-Pro NFL player, a Total
Tackle, and she, a Total Woman teacher. They've never
been happier together.

My Way

What causes most of the problems in your marriage? I
find that the conflict between two separate egos is usually

the culprit—your viewpoint versus his viewpoint. If they happen to be the same, fine. If not, as so often is the case, conflict results.

For instance, your weary man comes home from the office longing for a quiet evening. You've been cooped up in the house all day and want to get out. There's instant conflict with two egos, each shouting, "Me, me, me."

Or you have a little extra money. He wants that new car and you have your heart set on new carpeting. Conflict. He wants to go to the game Saturday and you want to go shopping. And so it goes.

Every couple has this problem. How can two different egos fuse their two different opinions into one? Some don't. Often these conflicts are "resolved" when the parties go their separate ways, instead of growing together.

The biblical remedy for marital conflict is stated, "You wives must submit to your husbands' leadership in the same way you submit to the Lord" (6). God planned for woman to be under her husband's rule. Now before you scream and throw this book away, hear me out.

First of all, no one says you have to get married. If you do not wish to adapt to a man, the negative implication is to stay single. If you are married but not adapting, you probably already know that marriage isn't the glorious experience you anticipated.

Secondly, you may think, "That's not fair. I have my rights. Why shouldn't he adapt to my way first, and then maybe I'll consider doing something to please him?" I have seen many couples try this new arrangement, unsuccessfully. Unless the wife adapts to his way of life, there's no way to avoid the conflict that is certain to occur.

Thirdly, please note that I did not say a woman is inferior to man, or even that a woman should be subservient to all men, but that a wife should be under her own husband's leadership.

Fourthly, another little phrase may cause some consternation: ". . . in the same way you submit to the Lord." Perhaps you are thinking, "I don't submit to the Lord. I don't even know Him. How archaic can you get? Even if you believe in Him, who submits to Him?"

The fact is that God originally ordained marriage. He gave certain ground rules and if they are applied, a marriage will work. Otherwise, the marriage cannot be closely knit because of the inherent conflict between your husband's will and yours. The evidence is all too clearly visible. In some cities there are now more people getting divorced each day than getting married.

Man and woman, although equal in status, are different in function. God ordained man to be the head of the family, its president, and his wife to be the executive vice-president. Every organization has a leader and the family unit is no exception. There is no way you can alter or improve this arrangement. On occasion, families have tried to reverse this and have elected a woman as president. When this order is turned around, the family is upside down. The system usually breaks down within a short period of time. Allowing your husband to be your family president is just good business.

Oh, King, Live Forever

I have been asked if this process of adapting places a woman on a slave-master basis with her husband. A Total Woman is not a slave. She graciously chooses to adapt to her husband's way, even though at times she desperately may not want to. He in turn will gratefully respond by trying to make it up to her and grant her desires. He may even want to spoil her with goodies.

Marriage has also been likened to a monarchy, where the husband is king, and his wife is queen. In a royal marriage, the king's decision is the final word, for his country and his queen alike. The queen is certainly not his slave, for she knows where her powers lie. She is queen. She, too, sits on a throne. She has the right, and in fact, the responsibility to express her feelings, but of course, she does so in a regal way. Though the king relies heavily on her judgment, if there is a difference of opinion, it is the king who makes the final decision.

Now hold on, I know just what you're thinking; remember, I've been through all of this, too. What if the king makes the wrong decision? Oh, that's a hard one, especially when you *know* you're right, and there are times when that is the case. The queen is still to follow him, forthwith. A queen shall not nag or buck her king's decision after it is decreed. Remember those speedy trials, gals!

In so many marriages today, the woman rules the roost.

In others, there are two coequal rulers, whose decisions often clash. In still others, only the fittest survive. None of these cases enhance romance. Emotions are sent plummeting to zero, and the husband is left wondering, "How did I get into this mess?"

A lawyer's wife told me after a class, "I wasn't brought up to adapt to any man; in fact, just the opposite. I was taught as a small girl that no man is to be trusted. Men are only out for what they can get, and if you shack up with one for life, do him before he can do you." Having this propaganda piped into her little computer as a child has certainly caused her great obstacles today.

I would like to say right here, that in the beginning I was as dubious as anyone about adapting. But wow, has my thinking changed! I see now that a man does not want a nagging wife, nor does he want a doormat. He wants one with dignity and opinions and spunk, but one who will leave the final decision to him.

On January 15, 1972, Margrethe Alexandrine Thorhildur Ingrid became Queen Margrethe II of Denmark. Since childhood she had been groomed for the task of being queen someday. She had the finest education, received military training, and was prepared in every way to be a queen.

Her husband, Prince Hendrik, has no function constitutionally, other than as husband of the queen. But it is no secret that Hendrik wears the trousers at home. "Ever since I was a little girl," Margrethe said on the day of her engagement, "I have believed that even though I must officially take first place, it would be possible for me to take second place in marriage."

If a real live queen who could *demand* subservience from her husband feels that way, can we queens do less?

Last October, Charlie wanted to go to a football game on the same night as the "wedding of the year." I wanted to attend that wedding very badly; I'm sure you know the feeling. But Charlie explicitly wanted me with him for the game. Wishing I were two people, I finally consented to go with him and not pout. Charlie knew it was a great sacrifice for me and he was sweet and gentle for days afterward. Later, I wondered to myself why he didn't say, "Go on to the wedding," when he knew how much I wanted to go. I still don't know, but I did what was right and that brought its own rewards.

Several weeks later, we disagreed over Thanksgiving weekend plans. Charlie wanted to stay home, work around the house, and play with the family; I wanted to get away for a few days. We discussed both alternatives but obviously we could only do one together. I finally agreed he should have fun on the weekend, and that whatever he planned, I'd do willingly and enthusiastically. To my great surprise he announced a few hours later, "Get packed, let's take off for a few days!"

Adapting is not always this easy, however, so lest you think I'm unreal, I must share an absolutely stupid personal experience. I'm not proud of it, but nevertheless, I did it.

On another vacation trip, friends invited us deep-sea

fishing. I was tired and wanted to sleep in the sun that afternoon, rather than make conversation on a boat. Charlie asked that I go with him, and I cried and pleaded not to. He said, "I'm not going without you. They asked both of us and we'll either do one or the other." Still I didn't budge. Here was my husband pleading for me to accompany him on a date, and I told him no.

I won. We didn't go fishing, but I can tell you it wasn't worth it. Yes, I sat by the pool all afternoon, but I was immersed in guilt because I had ruined the last day of our vacation. Worst of all, we didn't communicate in any sense of the word for the next three days. Later I apologized and he forgave me, but the hurt had to wear off. I believe I felt worse than he did and I hope I learned my lesson once and for all. What can be worth having a strained relationship with the one you love and live with?

Adapting to his activities, his friends, and his food is not always easy, but it's right. I know that now. And I know when I don't want to adapt, it's my problem, not his. Sometimes I tell him, "From your point of view, you're right, but from my point of view, I'm right. We may never agree, but I have to tell you how I feel." Crawling behind his eyeballs helps me understand how he feels. Sometimes it takes awhile to talk myself into adapting, but the benefits are so great. Much more important than presents are those priceless times of tenderness. Last week Charlie took my face in his hands and plastered gentle kisses all over it, the way I do to our baby's face. The sweetness of that moment encourages me.

Frilly Flannel PJ's

Carl and Betty had been married twelve years. Their first ten were a struggle financially, but then Carl acquired some sizeable government contracts and overnight their way of life changed. They bought a new ranch-style house. With his heady success, Carl told Betty enthusiastically, "Now we'll be able to travel and entertain more." But Betty was a quiet homebody who didn't like to travel. Nor did she want to entertain. When Carl wanted her to join him on a business trip to Germany, she refused to go, using the children as an excuse.

Betty is now divorced. She still lives in that lovely home with her two children. Carl has since found someone else to enjoy his exciting new way of life with him. In your marriage it only makes sense for both of you to paddle in the same direction. Otherwise, you'll only go in circles—or like Carl, he may pull out and go downstream.

Julie, a beautiful southern belle, was married to an outdoorsman who loved camping. She had never been the outdoor type and usually stayed home when Jim vacationed in the woods. She talked about her problem in class one day, and said, "I can't stand those jungle trips, but I'm going to go with Jim next time. I know how much he loves it."

That night, instead of curling up with her needlepoint while Jim worked on the camper, she joined him in the garage to keep him company. While he puttered around, she didn't say much, but stayed with him. The next day Jim came home with what he called "wonderful news." Julie thought he had sold the camper, but when she heard his announcement, she smiled weakly and gulped back her disappointment. Jim had just splurged and bought the best camper mattresses available!

Summer arrived and they packed up their three children on a cross-country camping trip. I wondered (or worried) about her from time to time until a beautiful picture postcard arrived from Wyoming about mid-July. It read:

So far, the Total Woman has survived bugbites, a broken foot, temperatures from one-hundred-four degrees to thirty-two degrees and now rain, with a smile. Makeup on the face every morning at 7:00 A.M. (ugh) and frills even on my flannel pj's—I am becoming a Total Woman. Finally, Jim has become a Total Man and we're staying in charming, warm, dry motels with running water and of all things—ELECTRICITY!

Yes, Let's!

Has your husband ever suggested what he thought was an exciting idea, and you responded, "Yes, but . . . ."? It may have been a simple request like, "Let's go bike riding after dinner," but you instinctively countered, "Yes, but . . . ." In doing so, you drenched or drowned his idea with your cold water. It doesn't matter what his idea was or what your excuse was; it had the same dreadful effect of challenging his leadership. He couldn't lead you; inwardly he resented that fact—and you.

You might not realize how many times you buck your husband on every subject. In fact, he may have clammed up years ago because of this very thing. The next time he makes a suggestion, respond if at all possible with an enthusiastic "Yes, let's!" You may have to pick him up off the floor, but the rewards for this can't be beat. If his suggestion doesn't appeal to you, you may need to call upon all your self-control not to blurt it out. While he's telling you his plan, decide to thrill him by accepting his idea graciously. If a friend had made the same suggestion, you might have gone along happily. Can you do less for your lover?

On vacations, Charlie and I have had more arguments about where to eat than about any other subject. When we didn't eat where I wanted to eat, I've been so upset I've nearly choked on the food. I have seen how my exclusive "right" to select the restaurant only brings us both indigestion.

Life is much easier when I simply tell him my preference, and then let him make the final decision, whether it's where we'll eat or where we'll live. If I can't support the plan, at least I'll support the man.

I tell Charlie, "It's your decision, I'll stand behind you whatever you decide." When I trust his judgment implicitly, I've found that he does not take advantage of me, whether it concerns a restaurant or a business decision. He's probably so grateful for the freedom of choice that he doesn't act foolishly. He weighs his decisions carefully, and often asks for my opinions. But when he doesn't, we have no barriers or cold war, just good communication.

Following the assignment to adapt to his way of living, Joan, a Palm Beach housewife, drove home eager to give it a try. She planned an elaborate steak dinner, complete with wine, candlelight and music. She soon found out, however, that even though the best-laid plans don't proceed according to script, the principle of adapting is still sound.

Joan first pressed her sexy red hostess gown and with hair in rollers, hopped into her bubble bath. Two minutes later the front door slammed, and in walked her husband —at four o'clock! She started to scream, "What are you doing home already?" but held it back. She was determined to adapt to his plans. When she kissed him warmly, he said, "What's for dinner? I'm starved. Let's eat right away." Poof went the seven o'clock candlelight dinner, but she dressed and hurried to the kitchen.

The sun was still shining when she lighted the candles and served the steak at 5:20. Abruptly at 5:45 her husband left the house for a card game with the boys. "I'll be home around midnight," he said. "Don't wait up for me."

Later in class, Joan told us how frustrated she had felt. "I was livid, but I held my tongue. Silently I cursed the Total Woman course, but as I walked him to the door, I vowed to give it one more try. I wanted so much to maintain a good attitude. I whispered in his ear, 'I'll miss you, honey. I'll be waiting for you when you get home.' Unbelievable as it sounds, he was home by eight o'clock that night and we had a glorious time together."

Sizzle at Ninety-Nine

At a recent football game, I overheard one wife say to another, "I know your husband is crazy about football. Are you a football nut, too?" The other wife smiled and replied, "I love my husband."

Mrs. Albert Einstein was asked, "Do you understand your husband's theory of relativity?" She smiled, "Oh, my, no, I just know how he likes his tea." That's love in a nutshell.

Although the name of Abraham is known throughout the earth as the founder of a great nation, a portion of this greatness must be credited to his wife, Sarah. 1 Peter 3:6 tells us if we follow in Sarah's steps, we will do well.

What did Sarah do that was so special? What makes her an example to follow? She was quite a remarkable gal, but she didn't start out that way. In fact, it took her a long time to wise-up! When she married Abe, her name was Sarai, meaning "contentious and vicious," a real nag. Although she was the local beauty queen, she had no beauty within. Many years went by before she got the message that making a good marriage a great marriage would rest largely on her.

God had told her to submit to Abe. At last, she decided to adapt to his way of life. She began to grant his every desire, and he returned the favors! She started calling Abe "lord." It wasn't his idea, it was hers. This change of attitude caused God to change her name to Sarah, which means "princess." What a change—from "vicious" to "princess." Their marriage started to sizzle when Sarah was ninety and Abraham was ninety-nine! And isn't it interesting that when Sarah started obeying Abraham, God gave them the son of promise, Isaac? Isaac means "laughter." There was no laughter in that home until Sarah adapted. Abraham so loved her calm and gentle spirit that when she died at one-hundred-twenty-seven years of age, he cried and mourned for days. He was inconsolable.

It is only when a woman surrenders her life to her husband, reveres and worships him, and is willing to serve him, that she becomes really beautiful to him. She becomes a priceless jewel, the glory of femininity, his queen!

7 *Appreciate Him*

I joined Charlie on a business trip to California some months ago. One evening we met before dinner at a Los Angeles law office. High atop the penthouse office overlooking Beverly Hills, the lawyer told us about his partner who had passed away six years before. "He was the most amazing and unforgettable person I ever knew," he said. "He was only fifty-nine when he died. Just before his heart attack, he shared some personal thoughts about life with me. He told me several times, 'As you grow older you'll find that the one thing to treasure most in life is loyalty, and the worst and hardest thing to accept is ingratitude.' "

The greatest attribute—loyalty. The worst—ingratitude. As I pondered the counselor's last words I realized they were, to a degree, opposites. Ingratitude is almost the antithesis of loyalty. This prominent California lawyer must have been burned more than once. The very statement implied that the cruel act of ingratitude had hurt him to the core.

Underdone or Overkill

Husbands, too, feel that deep hurt. One remarked to me, "Maybe it's the age we're living in, but everybody seems so unappreciative. And my wife heads the pack. There's just no joy in giving, mainly because she is so ungrateful." An ungrateful wife is no joy to her husband, yet so many wives are guilty of gross ingratitude. They have forgotten those simple words, "Thank you," and all the actions and emotions those words connote.

If your husband came home tonight and met you at the door with a box of candy or a bouquet of roses, what would be your first reaction—suspicion or warmth? I think many wives might not express appreciation but would, instead, react in one of the following ways:

a. She'd say, "Now where have you been?"

Translation: "You've been up to something and I'm suspicious!" Instantly her husband reads these vibrations. To him, she's the judge and he's suddenly on the stand. He feels guilty and condemned even if he came home with a clear conscience.

b. Or she'd say, "Well, it's about time!"

Translation: "I've deserved this for months. My efforts have been overlooked. You're long overdue." Her husband has now witnessed a transformation before his very eyes. His wife has become a creditor, and he's actually *owed* her the flowers for months. Instead of being a donor, he's been made a debtor.

c. Another might say, "Is this a rewrap or did the funeral home close early?"

Translation: "The price of your gift is in direct proportion to your love for me. I'd really love you for a biggie; but I can't get carried away over these flowers." The shell-shocked husband now sees his wife as the cashier, and he's the cheapskate who sheepishly paid for the smaller item in the store.

d. Finally, she might say, feebly, "Candy, how nice."

Translation: "Just what I don't need! You know I'm on a diet, dumb-dumb!" The husband now looks at Miss Insatiability in utter frustration. Everything he tries is a failure. He blew it again. He's incapable of fulfilling her desires.

More often than not a wife will react in one of these ways, all of which are examples of ingratitude. Occasionally, however, a wife will go overboard in the opposite direction, and say, with teeth showing, "Oh, dahling, I just love it!" But inside, she says to herself, "Smile, anyway."

Miss Overkill never fools anyone—especially her husband. He's seen the same fixed grin on a thousand other occasions. Her reaction is always the same, regardless of the motivation. It's merely ingratitude in a different disguise. Inside he feels unworthy of a true response from his wife.

Attitude of Gratitude

Stop a moment and check your gratitude meter. Are you guilty of that heinous act of ingratitude? Are you appreciative of the basics your husband knocks himself out to provide? Not just the birthday and Christmas "specials," but money for the groceries, doctor bills, and pillowcases?

Appreciation involves two parts—internal and external. First of all, a wife cannot be grateful if she's grasping for her rights. If she feels she has the *right* to be taken out to dinner once a week, she will not express sincere gratitude. Only if she yields this right to her Creator is she able to fully appreciate dinner out, since it is then a privilege, an unforgettable experience.

Secondly, appreciation from within must be communicated outwardly, by words, attitude, or action, or by all three. This is easy since a heart of gratitude must express itself. A thankful person cannot keep quiet.

Don't let your "rights" keep you from being grateful. Thank your husband for all those little things in life and he'll begin to give you those extras you've always wanted. Thank him for supporting the family. If you're a working wife, he especially needs your reassurance and appreciation, since his masculinity may be threatened by your paycheck.

Last Christmas, I watched as a husband shopped at a perfume counter. He told the saleslady, "Just hand me one of those gift packages. It doesn't matter what I buy for my wife as long as it's expensive. She'll bring it back anyway."

Then he smiled and said, "Now I'd like to pick out another gift. This is for my secretary. I love to see her reaction." He spent twenty minutes choosing the right one for her!

When a man gives his wife a present, his only reward is seeing how pleased she is. In one case, a husband gave his wife a bracelet, but it wasn't to her choosing. She took away his joy by constantly complaining about it. Finally she exchanged it for one she liked. Her husband hasn't bought her any gifts since, and why should he?

If you're not really crazy over a gift, be careful. If at all possible, try to use it. Express your appreciation for his taking time from his busy day. If you don't actually like the gift, don't be insincere and say you do. But you can still tell him how thoughtful he is for thinking of you, and be sure to thank him for the surprise.

Charlie told me about the morning he drove our three-year-old, Michelle, to her grandmother's house. As he dropped her off, Michelle kissed him good-bye and tenderly whispered, "Thank you, Daddy." Charlie felt like a king all day. Childlike appreciation lifts the heart. Daddies need that too!

The perfect balance between ingratitude and overkill is an attitude of gratitude. A sincere "Thank you, honey," by words and actions will satisfy any husband, whether it be for a mink stole or a bag of popcorn. That biblical admonition. "It is more blessed to give than to receive" (7), is so true. Don't keep your husband from being blessed!

I received a postcard recently from an alumna who had generously used the four A's—to accept, admire, adapt, and appreciate her husband. The card read:

> The Total Woman is in heaven—a beautiful suite over-looking the Atlantic Ocean in the heart of San Juan—new, gorgeous luggage in my closet, with the sweetest guy in the world as my companion. That course is powerful stuff! "Nothing's too good for my honey!" Bob says. Those four A's are the keys to making my man come alive!

Assignment

1. Accept your husband just as he is. Write out two lists—one of his faults and one of his virtues. Take a long, hard look at his faults and then throw the list away; don't ever dwell on them again. Only think about his virtues. Carry that list with you and refer to it when you are mad, sad, or glad.

2. Admire your husband every day. Refer to his virtue list if you need a place to start. Say something nice about his body today. Put his tattered ego back together with compliments.

3. Adapt to his way of life. Accept his friends, food, and life-style as your own. Ask him to write the six most important changes he'd like to see take place at your house. Read the list in private, react in private, and then set out to accomplish these changes with a smile. Be a "Yes, let's!" woman some time of every day.

4. Appreciate all he does for you. Sincerely tell him "Thank you" with your attitudes, actions, and words. Give him your undivided attention, and try not to make any telephone calls after he comes home, especially after 8:00 P.M.

Part Three
Sex 201

8 Painting the House

Let's begin by going back to that moment when you first saw the man who is now your husband. Specifically, let's consider the first time he saw *you*. Remember how immaculate you were each time he came to call? Remember those long baths and then the powder, perfume, and pizazz? You felt so confident, and you were so excited you could hardly wait to see him. Dazzling, you floated out to meet him, knowing he would be pleased just seeing you and being seen with you.

Well, what did you look like last night when he came home? What did you have on this morning when he left for work? Girls, is it any wonder the honeymoon is over, and instead of feeling sought, you both feel caught?

It doesn't have to be that way. You see, you are the one he wants to thrill. Remember, you are the one woman he selected to live with exclusively. He chose you from all the other girls. You are the one he wants to adore. In turn, you are the one who can send him into orbit any time you want.

Fizzle to Sizzle

One of your husband's most basic needs is for you to be physically attractive to him. He loves your body; in fact, he literally craves it. The outer shell of yours is what the real estate people call "curb appeal"—how the house looks from the outside. Is your curb appeal this week what it was five years ago?

Many a husband rushes off to work leaving his wife slumped over a cup of coffee in her grubby undies. His once sexy bride is now wrapped in rollers and smells like bacon and eggs. All day long he's surrounded at the office by dazzling secretaries who emit clouds of perfume.

This is all your husband asks from you. He wants the girl of his dreams to be feminine, soft, and touchable when he comes home. That's his need. If you are dumpy, stringy, or exhausted, he's sorry he came. That first look tells him your nerves are shot, his dinner is probably shot, and you'd both like to shoot the kids. It's a bad scene. Is it any wonder so many men come home late, if at all?

It was a wise woman who once said, "A man can stand about anything, except boredom." Is your husband bored? The quickest way to spin him around is to change your appearance. Will he be star-struck by the way you look tonight?

When you look smashing, you can forget yourself and

concentrate on the other person. In marriage, that's the name of the game—to concentrate on the other person!

Remember, fellow wives, a man thinks differently than we do. Before a man can care about who a woman is, he must first get past that visual barrier of how a woman looks. So your appearance at 6:00 P.M. should have top priority! Those first four minutes when he arrives home at night set the atmosphere for the entire evening.

Determine to be a charming atmosphere adjuster tonight. Greet him at the door with your hair shining, your beautifully made-up face radiant, your outfit sharp and snappy—even though you're not going anywhere! He'll feel more alive just coming home to you, when your whole countenance and attitude say, "Touch me, I'm yours!"

Happy Homecoming

If scene number two is for you, take a few extra moments for that bubble bath tonight. If he comes home at 6:00, bathe at 5:00. I know it sounds ludicrous if you have two little ones and four hungry mouths to feed by 6:07. That's my situation, but the bubble bath is part of my schedule anyway. Let the little ones' eyes gaze if they must, but treat yourself to a warm, sweet-smelling, relaxing bath. In preparing for your six o'clock date, lie back and let go of the tensions of the day. Think about that special man who's on his way home to you.

Remove all prickly hairs and be squeaky clean from

head to toe. Be touchable and kissable. For a really sparkling mouth, use dental floss after brushing your teeth, then brush again, and close with a good mouthwash. You could greet anyone after that!

Rather than make your husband play hide-and-seek when he comes home tired, greet him at the door when he arrives. Make homecoming a happy time. Waltzing to the door in a cloud of powder and cologne is a great confidence builder. Not only can you respond to his advances, you will also want to. And if he has come home cranky, it will be awfully hard for him to stay that way when you look and smell delicious!

Costume Party

One morning, Charlie remarked about the pressures of the day that lay ahead of him. All day I remembered his grim face as he drove away. Knowing he would feel weary and defeated, I wondered how I could revive him when he came home.

For an experiment I put on pink baby-doll pajamas and white boots after my bubble bath. I must admit that I looked foolish and felt even more so. When I opened the door that night to greet Charlie, I was unprepared for his reaction. My quiet, reserved, nonexcitable husband took one look, dropped his briefcase on the doorstep, and chased me around the dining-room table. We were in stitches by the time he caught me, and breathless with that old feeling of romance. Our little girls stood flat against the wall watching our escapade, giggling with delight. We all had a marvelous evening together, and Charlie forgot to mention the problems of the day.

Have you ever met your husband at the front door in some outrageously sexy outfit? I can hear you howl, "She's got to be kidding. My husband's not the type, and besides, we've been married twenty-one years!"

Nope, I'm not kidding, *especially* if you've been married twenty-one years. Most women dress to please other women rather than their own husbands. Your husband needs you to fulfill his daydreams.

I have heard women complain, "My husband isn't satisfied with just me. He wants lots of women. What can I do?" You can be lots of different women to him. Costumes provide variety without him ever leaving home. I believe that every man needs excitement and high adventure at home. Never let him know what to expect when he opens the front door; make it like opening a surprise package. You may be a smoldering sexpot, or an all-American fresh beauty. Be a pixie or a pirate—a cowgirl or a show girl. Keep him off guard.

You don't think you're the type? I didn't either. It took me seven years of marriage to try costumes on him. I only tried them then because my marriage needed some sizzle. But my silly costumes got such fabulous results that now I'm hooked. And so is Charlie. My first costume, the pink baby-dolls and boots, was among my more conservative outfits. For a corn-fed gal from a small Ohio town, I must admit I've branched out quite a bit since then!

You may not want a costume party every night, but you can work toward it. Keep a step ahead of your husband. Keep him guessing. If you have older children, naturally use discretion when they are around. You may not wish to parade around in nylon net at half-past five with your fifteen-year-old son all eyes. But the children will love your costumes. It makes life exciting. Can't you just imagine Junior on the sandlot telling his friends, "I've got to go now, guys. Got to see Mom's outfit for tonight."

One son came home from college while his mother was taking the course. He told her, "Mom, you look so cute lately. I hope I can find a woman like you for a wife."

Sophisticated Connie laughed out loud at the class assignment to dress up for the evening's homework. "I'm certainly not the type to put on any silly costume," she blurted out. "My husband would think it's ridiculous."

Later that week she and her husband attended his company's annual dinner-dance. One of the secretaries stopped the show with a most revealing gown. As Connie watched her husband's glassy eyes, she casually asked him, "What would you do if I wore a getup like that to greet you some night?" His reply was a shock to her. "Oh honey," he said, "I'd love it. If I thought you'd be home waiting for me in an outfit like that, the bumper-to-bumper traffic wouldn't bother me a bit. In fact, I might even leave early to beat the traffic!" Connie is a smart woman. She tried it. He liked it!

Another graduate appeared in a sheer black lace gown. Her husband was speechless when he opened the front door. The surprise element caught him completely off guard. She told me later that the evening was not only lots of fun, but he had also suggested a cruise to Nassau the following week!

Still another gal took the course being held in her Southern Baptist Church. She welcomed her husband home in black mesh stockings, high heels, and an apron. That's all. He took one look and shouted, "Praise the Lord!" He was flabbergasted, but extremely pleased. He could hardly eat his dinner!

One middle-aged woman who had been married for many years found this part of the assignment rather difficult. She ruled out the baby-doll route, but put on a new dress for dinner and said demurely, "Dear, I'm wearing my new dress with the no-bra look." Her husband couldn't quite believe it, but said, "This is one of the happiest moments of my life; I just don't want it to end."

These stories may sound unbelievably naive, but I can assure you that costumes bring a surefire response. Two last words of caution are suggested as you start: First, don't use costumes as a gimmick to manipulate your husband. He will sense it if you're not sincerely trying to please him out of love. Be sure your attitude matches your costume.

Anita Bryant, a Total Woman alumna, related some of her class experiences in her best-selling book *Bless This House*. When she took over the care of her twins, she and her husband Bob Green became so fatigued mentally and physically, that they had no energy or interest in sex.

"We reached a point where we didn't bother even to kiss goodnight," Anita wrote. "It kept bugging me that Bob didn't hold my hand or kiss me goodnight, but I was too proud to mention it. Besides, maybe some of it was my fault."

Recalling her class assignment to dress up for sex, Anita packed a new, sexy peignoir and determined to turn a two-day engagement in Houston into a mini-honeymoon! Enroute, however, travel plans went awry, and Anita began to nag Bob over the meals, flight reservations, and other assorted trivia. By the time her evening show was completed, Bob was worn and frazzled from her continued harassment.

Back at the hotel, Anita took time to prepare for her "late night" show for her husband. She entered the bedroom in what she called "the flattest grand entrance in history." Bob took one look, asked if the gown was one he had gotten her last Christmas, then turned over and went to sleep. Anita stayed up most of the night fuming at him for not responding to her advances.

The next day she confessed her frustration and disappointment to Bob, who told her, "I was still mad at you for all the complaining you had done. I didn't turn on because I knew it was supposed to turn me on."

Anita felt chagrined and humbled by the truth. "What does turn you on?" she asked.

Bob was silent for a moment and then said sternly, "Kindness, Anita." She realized then that a sexy outfit was only half the assignment; her attitude had not matched her costume.

Secondly, make sure you recognize your husband's car door or knock at the door when he arrives. Zealous to surprise her husband, a Fort Lauderdale housewife, dressed a la gypsy with beads, bangles, and bare skin, greeted the equally surprised water meter reader!

Recently I said to Charlie, "I wish I could be gorgeous and ravishing in the mornings when you leave but between breakfast and getting the girls off to school, I just can't." "That's okay," he grinned, "as long as you're gorgeous and ravishing when I come home."

Your husband will love it too. And he will love you for wanting to please him. When his need for an attractive and available wife is met, he'll be so grateful that he will begin to meet your needs. Try it tonight!

9 Rocks in the Mattress

Sex is the world's most popular theme. Billboards, magazines, and movies all scream out sex. Many fifth graders today can recite technical information about sex that would make their grandmothers blush. Doctors and scientists claim new discoveries daily and publish the results for the world to see. Sex books monopolize the best-seller lists. Most women's magazines carry a lead article on sex in each issue. No longer is sex a taboo that people discuss secretly.

Why then are so many women having more sex, but enjoying it less? Where's the fun in sex?

Columnist Ann Landers wrote recently that years ago, a prominent divorce lawyer told her nine out of ten divorces start in the bedroom. She didn't believe him at the time, but she does now. During her fifteen years of operating a supermarket confessional, she has found that when a marriage goes on the rocks, the rocks are usually in the mattress. In other words, if a couple has a really good sexual relationship, they will try a lot harder to work out their problems and stay married.

One such rock in the mattress is the sexless marriage. I heard one woman say, "We can't have sex because our teen-age daughter's room is next to ours. She might hear us!" I wondered how many years it had been for them. This story is not as unusual as it may sound. I know of many cases where intelligent married men and women forego sexual intercourse for months on end. The reasons are many and varied; the results are disastrous.

Ann Landers received another interesting letter from a thirty-five-year-old wife who had been married fifteen years and had three children. She wrote, "My husband is a nice fellow, and I like him a lot. But I want him as a friend from now on. I would appreciate it very much if he didn't bother me for sex anymore.

"I am not interested in anyone else, in case you are wondering. My husband is home every night and there is nothing wrong with him. He bathes regularly and we don't fight. I need to know if my way of thinking is all right. Please be frank and give me the straight facts."

Ann answered back, "It's all right with ME—but the question is, is it all right with your husband? If it is, you have no problem. The trouble starts when there is a difference of opinion."

I believe many women secretly feel this way. They would like to disregard sex and keep on playing marriage.

Alone Again, Naturally

A vivacious young mother confessed, "My husband gets a charge out of sex, but I've never had any fireworks. We've been married nine years, and have four children, but I guess I've never experienced a climax."

Many women believe that sex in marriage is just doing what comes naturally. If nothing comes naturally, the wife feels disillusioned. Soon she develops a defensive, "I couldn't care less" attitude. Her husband misinterprets that attitude and thinks she doesn't care about him anymore. Forlorn in this situation, he longs for romance. This is a dangerous state. A married man shouldn't be wandering around with an unfulfilled libido. A Total Woman knows that sex is vital to her marriage. Unless both she and he are satisfied during sexual intercourse, her marriage rates only a C+ at best.

Sex is not merely the joining of a man's and woman's sexual organs. It can and should be so much more. The Old English word for sexual intercourse is "to know." A man and wife are to know each other in the depths of their being.

Physically, the climax during intercourse is the greatest pleasure on earth. Medical research reveals that a climax renews and restores the body. Better physical health also results. What marvelous therapy!

Emotionally, a woman's climax, coupled with the joy she receives giving herself to her husband, completes her. She and her husband both feel satisfied and fulfilled.

Spiritually, for sexual intercourse to be the ultimate satisfaction, both partners need a personal relationship with their God. When this is so their union is sacred and beautiful, and mysteriously the two blend perfectly into one. Intercourse becomes the place where man and woman discover each other in a new dimension.

If any of these pieces of the puzzle are missing, this discovery is only partial. The partners may feel empty and lonely. They may feel restless, dissatisfied, and detached. Sex becomes frustrating to the wife, and even destructive. This inward frustration usually appears in other areas of her life. She may become a nagger, a screamer, or a whiner. And she would be fortunate if her problems only stopped there.

The Original Newlyweds

In the beginning, sex started in the garden. The first man was all alone. The days were long, the nights were longer. He had no cook, no nurse, no lover. God saw that man was lonely and in need of a partner, so He gave him a woman, the best present any man could receive.

Next to the rose bushes in the garden, God performed the first surgery, complete with anesthesia. He lifted a spare rib from his side and built a woman as man's instant companion. When the man awoke he was startled to see this strange creature looking at him. He rubbed his eyes, checked his ribs, and exclaimed, "Where have you been all my life?" (That's a rather loose translation. His actual words were, "This is now bone of my bones, and flesh of my flesh" [8].)

He sounded as though he were looking for someone to meet his needs, and now here she was. God told the newlyweds, "Multiply and fill the earth . . ." (9). Sex was for a twofold purpose: to express mutual love and to propagate the human race. There they were, man and woman before each other, naked and beautiful. They had no shame. Their human bodies were perfect. No bad parts; they were all good! They fit together perfectly in the exquisite relationship God had planned for them.

Because woman came out of man, he was incomplete without her, and she was incomplete without him. Thus they had the urge to merge! This was God's idea. What a great romantic. After all, He could have had them reproduce by rubbing noses! With no marriage manuals or doctors to consult, can't you imagine their fun and games experimenting with their newfangled parts?

This was the closest relationship possible on earth. Their sexual union had full blessing from God. He had conceived the idea by creating two sexes instead of one.

The Creator of sex intended for His creatures to enjoy it. We need never be ashamed to talk about what God was not ashamed to create. God viewed His creation and, "behold, it was very good" (10). It was good . . . it was good . . . it was very good.

Her Too?

If your sex life isn't satisfying, you can do something about it today. It may be that a change of attitude is all you need—or all he needs. It is surprising how ignorant so many husbands are concerning their wives' sex lives. In class one wife heard for the first time that she, too, should experience a climax. She went home and told her young executive husband, who replied, "I didn't think women were supposed to!" In this case some reeducation of both the husband and wife resulted in a revolutionized sex life. This couple also reported that certain tensions around the house virtually disappeared when the wife began to experience sexual satisfaction.

Men generally pride themselves on their sexual awareness, but your husband may not know how to satisfy you. *Sexual Happiness in Marriage* by Herbert Miles deals specifically with the physical mechanics of sex; you and your husband might find it helpful.

It may be, however, that your failure to climax is bound up in a deeper problem, either psychological or physiological. Attitudes that can affect your sex life or his are so varied that I could not possibly discuss them in this book. Indeed, many books have been written on this subject alone.

As you read, you may feel the need for professional help to reach the root of your problem. Don't be ashamed to seek help. There is no fault here. In fact, if you have a psychological hang-up, it probably started long before you were even aware of sex.

For example, your mother's attitude toward sex may have consciously or unconsciously influenced your attitudes. One grandmother admitted that she always thought intercourse was a sin because of Psalm 51, which reads, ". . . in sin did my mother conceive me" (11). For years this affected her relationship with her husband. She felt guilty about sex, even in marriage. She in turn passed on this concept to her children, whose lives were also affected. The ripples kept widening.

Only recently did she see that God devised sex for our pleasure, and that the verse in question refers to the sinful nature of mankind. All babies are born into sin by virtue of the fact that they are human. Another portion reads, "As by one man sin entered into the world, and death by sin; and so death passed upon all men, for that all have sinned" (12).

The Psalmist was actually saying that his mother was sinful because she was part of the human race, and he, too, had inherited this malady. Sex was not the first sin; man deciding to go his own way, rather than God's way, was the original sin. Sex was going strong before sin ever entered the world.

Lemonade Victoria?

One young bride who lived in the Victorian era recorded her innermost thoughts in a diary. She had never been alone with a man until she was married. Once during her courting days, the chaperone left the parlor for a few minutes to bring the lemonade. Her beau used that opportunity to snatch her hands, plant a fast kiss on her lips, and scoot back before the lemonade arrived.

Up until her wedding day, she and the boy, whom papa had picked out, had only touched hands and kissed a few times. On her wedding night, the new husband, whom she hardly knew, proceeded to consummate the marriage. The young bride recalled that night of lasting terror. To go from hand holding to intercourse in a few minutes was a shock, to say the least. Because of her strict standards, the young maiden considered it an actual rape. She never recovered from that first experience, and was never able to enjoy her husband's love. Preparation for that first night—proper sex education (and this does not mean premarital sex)—would have removed the fear of the unknown for her.

Today, with all of our advanced technology, women still pass on their sexual fears to their daughters. One girl told me how her mother counseled her before her wedding day. "You have to endure sex," she said. "It's a part of marriage. But never act as if you like it, because your husband will think you've been promiscuous."

Still other harmful attitudes toward sex keep cropping up. One divorcée told me, "Men are basically the enemy of women. They seek to subjugate and dominate, so we must compete. Men are simply animals, who want us for their own lustful desires." Her marriage lasted three rocky years.

To Hold, not Withhold

Dr. David Reuben, author of *Any Woman Can*, writes:

> Because emotions rule all sexual responses (including orgasm) a woman needs to review carefully her own personal attitudes about sex, her feelings about her husband and their relationship together. In some cases, the inability of having an orgasm is simply the unconscious refusal to have one, in order to get revenge on the husband.

Resentment toward a husband does not necessarily mean that he is at fault. It may be that the wife's real resentment lies against her father. After class a woman told me she felt rejected as a child because her father had left when she was seven. She had idolized him prior to that time and his departure shattered her emotionally. She passed on this suppressed hostility toward her father to all men in general, and specifically to her husband! "It broke my heart when my father ran off," she said, "and I guess I'm unconsciously making my husband pay for all the grief I've had."

When she understood what caused her basic distrust of men, she felt freed from that bondage of the past. Her husband noticed a different attitude immediately, and they began to mutually enjoy a new sexual relationship.

A young couple entered a psychologist's office for counseling and began to relate the drama of their marriage. They had begun dating as freshmen in college. Before long they were having relations together regularly. They married the summer after their sophomore year, and because of finances both of them quit school.

During the counseling session, it was obvious that the wife was intensely hostile toward her husband. Every dream in her life was smashed and she felt frustrated. She said, "Our life is a mess; nothing has worked out the way I thought it would, and it's all his fault."

"The husband had some faults and weaknesses," the psychologist said later, "but the real problem was her attitude. She blamed her husband for not controlling his passion before marriage, but couldn't admit that she could have said no. Now that she was married, she wouldn't let him touch her. She was subconsciously withholding sex because of her guilt feelings." After she saw her problem, they began to work together toward a solution.

Don't use sex as a weapon or a reward. Or, as the Bible says, "Do not cheat each other of normal sexual intercourse . . ." (13). God understood women. He knew they would probably use the prized possession of sex to manipulate men, and He warned against rationing it out. The Bible also states, ". . . let her breasts satisfy thee at all times; and be thou ravished with her love" (14). A wife is to love her husband constantly and unconditionally. Withholding sex in marriage as a form of punishment can only destroy the relationship.

On weekends, Marilyn did not see much of her husband, Bill, since he usually spent Saturdays and Sundays playing golf with his best friend, Justin. Marilyn resented Justin, and on weekends she resented her husband, too. When Bill came home from golfing, Marilyn punished him by refusing to make love.

In class, she learned that her husband needs other friends and recreation, just as she needs girl friends and luncheons. She also learned that her husband will not meet her needs when she withholds sex. Marilyn determined to change her attitude. The next time Bill was leaving to play golf, she said in a loving and understanding tone, "Have a good time, darling." Even though a flash of resentment briefly came back, she began to prepare herself for him while he was gone.

To her surprise, Bill came home early that day. He remarked that Justin had urged him to stay for dinner, but he had declined. Justin asked, "What's the matter, are you henpecked?" He replied, "No, I just want to get home to Marilyn!" So if this is your problem, hold him and don't withhold, and you may find your husband home early every night.

These examples show how far away from the bed sex problems can originate. Again, I encourage you to do whatever is necessary in your particular case to hang up your hang-ups, once and for all. Good sex is a must for a good marriage. With a sincere, open, and honest effort, you'll begin to enjoy the sexual pleasures you were meant to have.

Fireworks at Breakfast

A woman's most important sex organ is her brain. Unless her brain says, "Okay, go ahead," she cannot be fully satisfied sexually. No man can turn on a woman sexually unless she wants to be turned on. A middle-aged woman who had never experienced orgasm in years of marriage told me, "Finally, I let my brain say, 'Okay, go ahead,' and I had a brand-new attitude. Now I know for the first time why everyone is so excited about sex! This is the difference between just putting up with sex and really loving it."

Super sex is 20 percent education and 80 percent attitude. Your knowledge of sex may not be a problem, but your attitude may hang you up. Fortunately, your attitude can change.

That great source Book, the Bible, states, "Marriage is honourable in all, and the bed undefiled . . ." (15). In other words, sex is for the marriage relationship only, but within those bounds, anything goes. Sex is as clean and pure as eating cottage cheese.

Dr. David Reuben writes:

> Exotic sexual techniques are not nearly as important to
> a man as the knowledge that his wife loves him, cares
> about him and wants him sexually. The woman who does

her best to meet her mate's sexual needs goes a long way toward making him immune to the allure of other women.

The foundation for sexual happiness—or misery—is laid not in the bedroom, but at the breakfast table. The words a wife says or doesn't say to her husband as he leaves for work in the morning can determine what will happen that evening. The husband who feels right about sharing his innermost fears and hopes with his wife will probably never feel right about sharing his bed with anyone else. Those fleeting moments of orgasm in the darkness of the night are inseparably linked with all the mutual shared experiences throughout the day, the week, the year. Once a woman understands that completely, she has a powerful weapon against infidelity. . . . The wife who refuses to give her husband reasonable sexual satisfaction is literally asking him to go elsewhere.

Your husband wants a warm, comforting, and eager partner. If you're stingy in bed, he'll be stingy with you. If you're available to him, you need not worry about him looking elsewhere. Fulfill him by giving him everything he wants, and he'll want to give back to you.

It may take time for you to reach the closeness you desire with your husband. Don't be disappointed with yourself or him. With the proper attitude you'll improve. You'll find that sexual pleasure oils your marriage and helps keep it running smoothly.

You may not think of yourself as the last of the red-hot lovers, but your husband wants to. Deep down inside,

he's thinking, "How am I doing as a lover?" If you anticipate and enjoy sex, your husband will be confident as a
lover. This confidence will carry over to his work. He'll
be ready to tackle the world, with his battery charged,
and more bounce to the ounce.

Love in marriage is commitment. Commitment involves
a woman's full surrender to her man. You may not lose all
inhibitions overnight, but in time you can. Mental freedom
will give way to physical freedom, and the fireworks will
start!

10 Super Sex

Sex is an hour in bed at ten o'clock, super sex is the climax of an atmosphere that has been carefully set all day. Your attitude during your husband's first four waking minutes in the morning sets the tone for his entire day. The atmosphere for love in the evening can be set by you even before breakfast. Give him a kiss first thing tomorrow morning. Rub his back as he's waking up. Whisper in his ear. Slip into the bathroom to clear a few cobwebs before he wakes.

Remember, he can stand almost anything but boredom. The same nightgown month after month is not too exciting to any man. Treat him and yourself to some snazzy new ones. Have you ever looked so sexy in the morning that your husband called in late to the office? At least you can make him wish he could stay home.

One wife changes the sheets every few days while her husband is dressing for work. As she sprays the sheets with cologne, she purrs, "Honey, hurry home tonight." It gives him incentive for the whole day. If you expect great sex tonight, it should definitely start in the morning, with words. That's basic. Sex 201.

Edna St. Vincent Millay wrote, " 'Tis not love's going hurts my days, but that it went in little ways." Marriage is but a basketful of those little things.

Tomorrow morning as your husband leaves for work, stand at the door and wave until he's out of sight. That's his last memory of you, in the open doorway. Make him want to hurry home.

In class recently, one cute girl I'll call Janet told how she had anxiously anticipated her husband's coming home one day. At four o'clock she called his office somewhat nervously and said, "Honey, I'm eagerly waiting for you to come home. I just crave your body."

Jack said, with great consternation, "Ummmmmmph."

"Is there someone there with you, darling?" she asked.

"Ummhum," came the same reply.

"Well, I'll see you soon, darling," she said.

"Ummhum," was his final utterance.

And they both hung up.

Five minutes later the phone rang. It was Jack. In unbelief he said, "Would you please repeat slowly what you said five minutes ago?"

The sequel to the story was almost as amusing. Janet called her girl friend, Barbara, to tell what had happened. Barbara couldn't wait to try it on her husband, Pete. She called his office number and when the male voice answered, she said, "Darling, I wanted to call to say that I just crave your body. Hurry home!"

The voice on the other end demanded, "Who is this?" Realizing that another man, not her husband, had answered the phone, Barbara quickly hung up, absolutely mortified.

That night when her husband came in the door, he said, "Wait until I tell you about Ron's phone call today. You'll never believe it!" (She never told him, by the way, who the anonymous caller had been.)

So when you call your husband's office, first be sure you've got the right man! Then keep it short, just long enough to let him know that you're ready and willing. It may be the greatest news he has heard all day.

Luncheon Special

If you pack your husband's lunch in the morning, try tucking in a surprise love note. Mail a beautiful card to his office (marked PERSONAL) that would brighten up his day. Or appear in person. I know of one woman who arrived at her husband's office at lunch hour with a picnic-basket. Behind locked doors they spent the longest lunch hour the boss had taken in months. The secretaries are still talking about that one!

Arrange your day's activities so that you'll be totally and eagerly prepared as he walks in the door. A psychiatrist told me, "Lots of men would be less preoccupied

with work—or other women—if their wives made coming
home the most exciting part of the day."

I find that after a hard day at the office, most husbands
don't usually arrange flowers and light the candles in the
bedroom. At least mine doesn't, but he appreciates my
efforts. And it's my privilege to do it.

Set an atmosphere of romance tonight. Set your table
with cloth, flowers, and silver. Prepare his favorite dinner
for him. Eat by candlelight; you'll light his candle!

Make up your mind to be available for him. Schedule
your day so you won't start projects at nine o'clock. The
number-one killer of love is fatigue, but you won't be
exhausted if you're using your $25,000 plan. You'll have
the energy to be a passionate lover.

Next, be sure the outside of your "house" is prepared.
Bubble your troubles away at five o'clock. Of course,
you'll be shaven, perfumed, and seductive in an utterly
lovely outfit. Perhaps you're thinking, "Since I'm forty
pounds overweight, I don't feel very seductive in my
baby-doll pajamas." That's all right, he chose you because
he loves you. Concentrate on your good points and he
will, too. He won't be able to take his eyes off you. Best
of all, he'll know how much you care.

Prepare now for intercourse tonight. This is part of our
class assignment. In fact by the second week, the women
are to be prepared for sexual intercourse every night for
a week. When I gave the homework in one class, a woman
muttered audibly, "What's she think I am, a sex maniac?"

Another gal told a Total Woman teacher, "I tried to follow the assignment this past week, but I just couldn't
keep up—I was only ready for sex six nights; Monday night
I was just too tired." The teacher gave her a B—; but her
husband gave her an A!

One Fort Lauderdale housewife told how she diligently
prepared for love for seven straight nights, "whatever,
whenever, and wherever," and it was her husband who
couldn't take it. "I don't know what's happened to you,
honey," he said with a weak grin, "but I love it!"

Secrets of a Mistress

In the book *How to be a Happily Married Mistress,* the
author, Lois Bird, asks, "Would he pick you for his mistress? A mistress seduces. A housefrau submits. We all
know who gets the most goodies."

I don't approve of a mistress in any way, but maybe we
ought to check out the competition occasionally and see
why she is competition. Nell Kimball, a madame from a
bygone era, published her memoirs. She told about the
call girl, who is always bathed, perfumed, curled, and
adorned. She is never seen in bright lights, only dimly lit
rooms and candlelight. She never refuses her body or
talks about her headache. She never criticizes or belittles.
He is always the boss. She builds up his ego. She makes
sex exciting.

What about it, girls? Are you in a marriage rut? Would
your husband pick you for his mistress?

What made Marilyn Monroe the angel of sex? Why was she so desirable and delectable to tens of millions of American males? Norman Mailer, in his book *Marilyn*, writes: "She looked then like a new love ready and waiting between the sheets in the unexpected clean breath of a rare sexy morning, looking like she'd stepped fully clothed out of a chocolate box for Valentine's Day, so desirable as to fulfill each of the letters in the word of the publicity flack, *curvaceous*, so curvaceous and yet without menace as to turn one's fingertips into ten happy prowlers. Sex was, yes, ice cream to her. 'Take me,' said her smile, 'I'm easy. I'm happy. I'm an angel of sex, you bet.' "

A secretary interviewed by the *Miami Herald* about extracurricular activities between the girls in the office and their bosses was asked, "Do men at the office ever talk much about their wives?"

"Hardly ever," she said. "In all the time I've worked in an office I've never heard a man say, 'I'm married to the best woman in the whole world.' I'm always surprised when a wife comes into the office. She never looks as good as her husband. I think men get better looking with age. But, unfortunately, women don't.

"That's why a woman, it seems to me, has to work extra hard—make a real effort—to be an exceptional wife. To be considerate, attentive, as attractive as she possibly can be, especially when her husband is 35 or 40. She wouldn't get up in the morning and serve him breakfast looking like a witch if she knew how the girls in the office look. She'd be a lot nicer to him in everything she did. She'd try to live in his world."

Remember that the tone for the evening is set during the first four minutes after your husband comes home tonight. His senses will be anticipating food and sex. If he wants to make love tonight, love him extravagantly and wastefully. If you pour out your love on him unconditionally, he'll want to love you in return.

If you are suddenly overprepared for sex after months of denial, don't take it as a personal rebuff if he reacts with apparent disinterest, preoccupation, or suspicion Perhaps he needs to trust you. Be prepared and patient, it won't be long.

Perfect Wave of Libido

Has it ever dawned on you that making love in bed with the lights out, week after week and month after month might have become dull to your husband? To prepare your face for love, but not the time and place for love, rates only B−. If the bedroom is your only solution, at least make it romantic. An ancient book on love says fresh flowers are a must. So is music. Spray your sheets with sweet cologne. Immerse him in love.

For a change tonight, after the children are in bed, place a lighted candle on the floor, and seduce him under the dining-room table. Or lead him to the sofa. How about the hammock? Or in the garden? Even if you can't actually follow through, at least the suggestion is exciting. He may say, "We don't have a hammock." You can reply, "Oh, darling, I forgot!" If you are creative and imaginative, he'll love you for it.

For you boating enthusiasts, one smart wife packed a picnic supper and she and her husband shoved off for a late-night cruise. She said it was one of their most exciting evenings of married life. "Just searching for that perfect wave—of libido!" she said.

A Houston doctor gave this advice to a young wife: "I see that you're following the same pattern many of my older patients have followed. Most of them are wealthy, social, and very talented. All of them feel unfulfilled and all of them are neurotic. They are past the point of taking my advice, but you are young and can change the path you are on. My advice is this: Love your husband first and foremost. And, most important of all, don't ever love him at night!" What a startling prescription! This doctor knew that boredom sets in when sex becomes routine. He told her to make love in the morning or afternoon, not in the 10:30 rut.

Mrs. Mackey Brown analyzed why her marriage ended in divorce and told what she could have done to prevent it in an article titled "Keeping Marriage Alive through Middle Age," in *McCalls* magazine. "He found my love-making unimaginative . . . surely it would be better to use one's imagination to seek alternatives, solutions to live afresh before it is too late," she advised. "We never sneaked small vacations away from the children; sex became a bedroom ritual, almost meaningless except as a tension reliever. We never even went out for a quiet dinner alone, to say, 'Who are you and how are you?' When our grown-up children left home, we were left to stare astonished across the breakfast table, strangers in a stranger land."

Dr. David Reuben agrees.

The woman who would never think of serving her husband the same frozen television dinner every evening sometimes serves him the same frozen sexual response every night. Sex, like supper, loses much of its flavor when it becomes predictable. That, of course, is the lure of the other woman; she offers the illusion that sex with her will be different. But if a wife is on the same emotional wave as her husband it will be hard for anyone else to provide greater satisfaction.

Dr. George W. Crane, syndicated columnist, wrote, "Successful wives are superb boudoir actresses for they realize it is vital to serve as a one-wife harem to their mates! Boudoir cheesecake involves a lot of romantic histrionics!"

Just Undersupplied

For super sex tonight, respond eagerly to your husband's advances. Don't just endure. Indifference hurts him more than anything. He may enjoy making love even when you're a limp dishrag, but if you're eager, and love to make love, watch out! If you seduce him, there will be no words to describe his joy. Loving you will become sheer ecstasy.

The proverbs in the Bible speak much of married love. In modern paraphrase, one portion reads, "Man is to be intoxicated continually with the delight and ecstacy of his wife's sexual love" (16). I know of one instance where a psychiatrist advised a husband to be "continually intoxicated," literally. He was advised to have intercourse fourteen times a day! And you think you have problems! His wife said he was oversexed; he said he was just undersupplied. That was one man who was willing to follow his doctor's orders to the letter, even if it killed him. He said at least he'd die with a smile on his face.

Sexual intercourse is an act of love. Express your love by giving him all you can give. A woman's hands should never be still when she is making love. By caressing tenderly, you assure him that he's touchable. Tell him "I love you" with your hands.

Psychological test results reveal that infants who are not touched lovingly suffer emotional deprivation as adults. This basic need to be loved, touched, and comforted continues throughout life, in your life and his. He depends on you to reassure him that he's desirable to you. He needs confidence in this area where he may be vulnerable.

Your husband wants you to want him sexually. He wants you to enjoy lovemaking as much as he does. If you fail in this area, he is devastated. Down inside, he feels he is an utter failure. Believe in him and tell him so. Let him know he's your special project in life.

The Speed Demon

Tonight, as you make love, remember that your brain is your control center. Keep it tuned to the subject at hand. Think about his body, not Sunday's dinner menu. One of the secrets of life is to concentrate on the moment. Enjoy the present—not yesterday, or tomorrow, but right now! It's a secret to super sex, too.

In the same way you need words for atmosphere, so does he. Don't clam up. The silent-movie days are gone. He'll respond to your sounds of love. He does not automatically know what pleases you and what you don't like. The only way he'll know is for you to tell him. His enjoyment will be increased when he knows what is pleasing you. Tell him you want him. Treat him as if he is a great lover, and he'll become a great lover.

If your husband is a speed demon in sex and spends only a few minutes with you, your change in attitude will help slow him down. He will want to spend more time loving you. By seeing how you care, he will also want to see that your needs are met.

One important note—don't douse his flame of love once the romance begins. Any little negative word from you, even indirectly, may turn him off completely. If he senses you're not with him in the moment, he will be less than satisfied. He'll read it as a smoke screen or a cop-out.

Don't break the mood. Tell him tomorrow about that dented fender. Don't ask if he locked the back door. Hold back any sentences that start, "By the way." Watch your negative responses and diversions. Sometimes they're subtle and sometimes they're not. Any husband can pick up the vibrations of the more obvious ones like, "Oh, not again," or "Must we?" Others are more difficult to interpret, like, "Not tonight, my head hurts!" A headache on Monday night may be serious or subtle. A headache all week, however, may be very serious, but not very subtle.

Sometimes your passion is not as great as his, but you can still be warm and responsive. Love him whenever he wants to, if you possibly can. If you must refuse, be very gentle. Let him know you are not rejecting him, but you are willing to meet his needs in other ways.

Companion, not Competition

Sex can restore a bad mood or disagreement. One wife felt she had been wronged by her husband. Her pride took over and she refused to give in until he changed. The Bible advises, ". . . let not the sun go down upon your wrath" (17). Watch that no bitterness or resentment takes root in you for it causes deep trouble.

Nip it in the bud. Don't let your grudge carry over to the next day. There is no place for resentment in a good marriage. Part of his problem may be his need for your sexual love. Talk it out and change your attitude. Often that's all it takes.

Love never makes demands. Love is unconditional

acceptance of him and his feelings. He does not need competition at home; he's had that all day at work. He needs your companionship and compliments instead.

A mature couple does not demand perfection. They do not chase false goals, which can only end in disillusionment. They are willing to work together for each other's good, which produces a happy sexual adjustment.

Don't deprive your husband of intercourse when he acts like a bear. He may be tired when he comes home tonight. He needs to be pampered, loved, and restored. Fill up his tummy with food; soothe away his frustrations with sex. Lovemaking comforts a man. It can comfort you too.

In speaking to a men's service club recently, I told them some of the class assignments for super sex. The reason for the homework, I explained, was that sex comforts a man. The reaction of the men was completely unexpected. These sophisticated businessmen spontaneously shouted, pounded the tables, picked up their spoons, and clanged their water glasses!

Lovemaking is an art you can develop to any degree, according to *How to be a Happily Married Mistress*. You can become a Rembrandt in your sexual art. Or, you can stay at the paint-by-numbers stage. One husband, by the way, felt his wife was more like Grandma Moses because she always wore a flannel granny gown. The benefits in your becoming a Rembrandt just cannot be overemphasized. You can begin to be a budding artist today! Tonight is your night for super sex. Prepare, anticipate, and enjoy!

Assignment

1. Be an atmosphere adjuster in the morning. Set the tone for love. Be pleasant to look at, be with, and talk to. Walk your husband to the car each morning and wave until he's out of sight.

2. Once this week call him at work an hour before quitting time, to say, "I wanted you to know that I just crave your body!" Then take your bubble bath shortly before he comes home.

3. Thrill him at the front door in your costume. A frilly new nighty and heels will probably do the trick as a starter. Variety is the spice of sex.

4. Be prepared mentally and physically for intercourse every night this week. Be sure your attitude matches your costume. Be the seducer, rather than the seducee.

5. If you feel your situation involves a deeper problem, either psychological or physiological, seek professional help.

Part Four
Building Bridges

11 Reopening Clogged Lines

Charlie came home one Friday afternoon with a scowl on his face. I could tell it had been one of those days. We were invited out to dinner that evening, so I was cheery and effervescent. Refusing to allow him to dampen my evening, I chatted lightly. He glowered at me and then acted as if I weren't even in the room. Since there was no reason for him to be mad at me, I began to feel irritated. I finally quit trying to be nice, and we dressed in silence.

On the way to the party, I sat as close to my car door as I could, hurt by the icy barrier between us. I thought resentfully to myself, "If only I weren't teaching that blasted course, I'd tell him a thing or two."

About then we arrived at the party and, putting on the masks of society, gaily exuded, "Hi, how *are* you? We're just *fine*." Each couple seemed extremely *fine* and bright as they came in and I wondered if they were all mad at each other, too.

We didn't say two words to each other at the party, but on the way home, I thought to myself, "Wait a minute, what's happening here? We're civilized Americans and we're both over twenty-one. We shouldn't be acting like little kids. Charlie's had a bad day at the office, and he needs my love now more than ever." I said softly to him, "You've had a busy day and this has been such a hectic season. It's just caught up with both of us."

That little remark seemed to release the pressure and Charlie began to talk. Out tumbled all the thoughts that had been swirling around inside him. I was ecstatic to discover again that "A soft answer turneth away wrath" (18). Furthermore, that soft answer set the tone for the next day. Charlie announced at breakfast, "I feel such love for my fellow man this morning!" By talking out his frustrations the night before, he now felt understood. He was full of love, eager to pour it out on his world.

Silence is Stubborn

Robert Louis Stevenson wrote, "Marriage is one long conversation, chequered by disputes." Good communication is so essential for a good marriage, but all too often this ingredient is sadly missing. I am reminded of a cartoon which depicted a primitive caveman and woman looking at each other. Miss Cavewoman said, "Now that we've learned to talk, try to speak the same language!"

We women are so different from that strange but wonderful male species. Often we start from totally different premises when we try to communicate. A man talks to his wife so he can express ideas and information. A woman wants to talk about feelings and emotions. For instance, when was the last time you asked your husband, "Do you love me?" You *know* he loves you. He's told you so, hasn't he, but you have an emotional need to hear it again and again and again.

A woman expresses her love by words and expects words in return. A man expresses his love by actions—by sexual intercourse, bringing home the paycheck, or buying his wife a house. She wants words and tenderness; he gives her material goods. Is it any wonder we sometimes have trouble communicating?

An understanding woman is in great demand. Understanding the one you live with and love with gives such freedom. Give your husband that freedom and luxury and he'll adore you for it. Your marriage will begin to sizzle, and that's a promise.

Happier and Healthier Husbands

Love cannot take distance. A husband and wife must communicate if they hope to understand each other. There is no greater feeling than knowing you are understood. You feel confident, your burden is lifted, and you're ready to tackle the world.

Is your marriage line of communication clogged from underuse? The flow may be just slightly hindered, or it may be shut down to only a few drips. You can be a communication plumber, and your husband's psychotherapist as well, with the end result a happier and healthier husband. I hope you'll find these suggestions as therapeutic for your husband as they have been for mine:

1. *Be a good listener.* Whenever Charlie began talking at a dinner party, for years I thought that was my cue to begin talking to the person next to me. Around the house I wasn't much better either. I read magazines while he was talking, or I worked on other projects and only gave him half my attention. Naturally I missed much of what he was trying to tell me. I thought I could both read and listen and save time besides!

I found out, by trial and error, that Charlie was hurt by my indifference. He wanted me to look at him, concentrate on him, and hang on every word. He wanted me to listen to his stories, even though I'd heard them a dozen times before. He, like most husbands, wanted me to be his number-one fan, and prove it by being a good listener.

One night, he asked me to listen to his argument for court the next morning. Not just once, but three times, he presented his case. For over an hour I sat. He didn't want me to sew or look at magazines; he wanted my undivided attention. So I adored him as I listened, my eyes transfixed on his face. When he spoke a particularly brilliant phrase, I beamed. When the language was over my head, I frowned and pondered. I found myself actually enjoying his speech.

The next morning I could tell he felt confident about appearing in court. At breakfast he told the girls, "Let's all kiss Mommy. Everyone around the table to kiss Mom!" My day was made!

Douglas L. Steer said that to listen another's soul into a condition of disclosure and discovery may be almost the greatest service any human being ever performs for another. Anyone will talk but only true friends listen. If you're in doubt about this, observe your friends at the next party you attend.

Communication is sharing, not shoving. It involves two parts—talking and listening, and it involves at least two persons—the speaker and the listener. Both are vital in marriage. You must talk to communicate your thoughts, but you must also listen as your husband expresses his thoughts. When a husband says, "My wife doesn't understand me," he usually means, "She doesn't listen."

When Joe came home for dinner, he bounded in the door and exclaimed, "Guess what, honey? I finally landed the Miller Company order. Boy, what a mess that's been the past two months, but what a relief now. I've been on the phone to New York for three straight hours today locking up the contract."

Instead of responding, Ann answered, "Say, did you remember to pick up my package?" She was preoccupied and hadn't heard a word Joe had said. He wasn't simply saying that the order was difficult; he was saying, "I'm proud of my accomplishment. How about a pat on the back, Ann? Aren't you proud of me?" He was seeking recognition and a compliment from his wife.

Listen between the lines as your husband talks. You

may hear certain needs that will never be spoken audibly. If he has clammed up, don't pry; instead try complimenting him, and watch how he responds automatically. If he is relaxing in peace, keep still. If he talks, concentrate and listen.

2. *Don't give him advice.* Shakespeare warned, "Those who school others, oft should school themselves." All too often wives give loads of unsolicited advice, such as, "Well, Bob . . . if I were you . . . it seems to me . . . just looking at it logically . . . why don't you go in there tomorrow and fire him!" By advising him, he thinks you're condemning him and holding him responsible for the problem. Even though your intentions are good, you come off sounding like a second mother. He feels like a shamed little boy.

Who's running this ship, anyway? Save your lectures. He doesn't need your advice or your leadership in times of trouble. He needs your ear, not your mouth. One man hid behind his newspaper for thirteen years to avoid a face-to-face encounter with his wife. He was afraid she'd tell him what to do.

3. *Don't criticize or put him down.* At a dinner party, I heard a wife tell her husband across the table, "That's not a bad idea considering it's an original from your brain!" In another case, a glum husband told his wife he hadn't gotten the raise he had expected. His wife snapped, "I figured you wouldn't get it; you've always been a loser." With friends like that, who needs enemies! What man would tell his sarcastic wife what's really in his heart? If

he knows he'll be gunned down if he opens his mouth, he may either clam up completely or play the same game by dishing it back.

We women are so prone to criticize and put our husbands down, especially at parties and with friends. Life is far too short for playing these games. They're not cute, they're cruel, and they build bitter walls which only hinder effective communication.

4. *Understand his frame of reference.* Often our best moments are not when we're shooting down contrary opinion, but rather allowing it to be spoken. We can never understand that which we never hear. Mutual understanding is only possible through bilateral communication.

The next time you and your husband are in a verbal deadlock, stop and consider his frame of reference. Once you understand his basic premise, you'll find that his conclusions are logical from his point of view. Every man (or woman) is logical if you simply understand the base from which he operates.

One afternoon, Chad Jones was driving in the Colorado mountains with his wife, testing the maneuverability of his new sports car. As he was negotiating a turn at high speed, his wife's endurance stretched to the breaking point. She held her breath, and then slammed her foot to the floorboard, unconsciously trying to stop the car. She grabbed Chad's arm, which had a firm grip on the steering wheel, and screamed, "Stop, Chad, we're going to be killed!"

They made the curve, and she cooled off after a few

moments, but not Chad. He kept thinking, "That wife of mine almost caused a wreck." But the more he thought about it, the more he realized that her logic was not all that bad. He had driven in the mountains for years without an accident. His base was, "I've made these curves for years, and chances are I'll make this one. Experience lessens the chance of accident." Her base was, "You've made those curves for years without an accident, and according to the law of averages, you're long overdue." Both conclusions were logical but based on different premises.

A husband told his wife that he'd like to take some evening courses for his job. His wife's first thought was "Oh, no, you're not home enough as it is, and now you'll be gone two more nights a week." But instead of complaining or discouraging his idea, she crawled behind his eyeballs and saw it from his viewpoint. "He doesn't want to escape from the house," she realized. "He just wants to be the best man in the office."

After she thought it through, she said sincerely, "Honey, I'm proud of you for wanting to be the best informed man on your job. I know it won't be an easy schedule for a while, but I'm all for it." She saw it as he saw it, and her encouragement was just what he needed.

5. *Be sensitive to his moods.* Ron and Marie had a fight at breakfast as usual. Ron felt discouraged while driving to work, but then pressed it down. When he arrived at the office, he had a run-in with a disgruntled but important customer. Then the boss came in fuming over a technical

error Ron had made. As the boss left, he stopped and chatted with that younger man next door, Ron's competitor.

All day long, Ron felt old and threatened. When he came home, he asked Marie to run a few errands. She sighed, "I can't go right now, I've got some other things to do." Ron's bruised ego picked up the signals. He felt worthless. He wanted to crawl into his shell and lock the door.

Your husband may have crawled into his shell. He needs you to look for the good in him. Encourage him. Tell him, "You have the ability to do the best job that's ever been done. I have confidence in you that you'll do it!" And he will!

When your husband comes home after one of those days and takes it out on you, be sensitive to his moods. Coldly diagnose his problem and then treat him warmly. Remember that he probably felt threatened that day at the office. He can't sit down and cry actual tears; but he may be crying inside, so his emotional reaction may come out as anger toward you. He needs your comfort and warmth now, more than ever. Don't prod or whine if he doesn't open up to you. Communication may not occur instantly, especially if it hasn't been free-flowing for some time. He may not talk if he cannot trust you. Are you trustworthy?

6. *Be interested in his interests.* I never read the sports page before we were married, but it wasn't long before I noticed what section my husband grabbed first each

morning. So I decided to read it myself, out of curiosity at first; out of love later on.

One morning, I read about a football player who had just been traded. I memorized his name and practiced saying it all afternoon. At dinner, I casually asked Charlie what he thought about the Dallas Cowboys' new trade for this player. In disbelief he dropped his fork and slowly looked up at me. He couldn't believe I had read the article, but he really appreciated my being interested in his interests.

If your husband is a football nut like mine, learn about his game. If he thrives on prehistoric woodpeckers, make an effort to converse on prehistoric woodpeckers. Care enough to be interested in what interests him. Be that real friend!

Cooling a Hothead

My marriage, like yours, has its problems from time to time. There is no perfect marriage or perfect husband, just in case you were still searching. Problems are normal and no marriage is immune, so cheer up. The variable, however, lies in how you cope or fail to cope with disagreements when they arise. For example, how do you react when you're mad at your husband? Do you explode volcano style, or do you keep your frozen rage inside? Either way can be dangerous and unhealthy.

Too many women push their anger down inside and pretend it's not there. But the silent treatment, instead of resolving conflict, only intensifies it and turns molehills into mountains. Playing the silent martyr takes tremendous power, and anger is usually the source of that power. The price of silence is too high. First of all, it cuts off communication completely, and secondly, your body pays the price. The angry but silent wife tends to relive the problem over and over, each time trying to further justify her position. At night she may share the same bed with her husband, yet feel a million miles apart. Lying there she feels wronged and bitter, especially when he goes to sleep before she does!

The Bible says, ". . . let not the sun go down upon your wrath" (19). Don't let roots of bitterness spring up (20), but instead, take care of your conflicts day by day. Burdens carried over to the next day are too heavy to handle. Roots of bitterness become a poison within your body. They affect your everyday thoughts and actions, eat away at your facial expressions, and can even cause physical illness.

Sophisticated society has conditioned us to be deceitful through the art of trite cliches, forced smiles, and facades. In a healthy marriage, however, there should be neither deceit nor secrets. Both husband and wife should feel free to express their honest feelings by using tact, not attack. The next time you lock horns with your husband, try these helpful suggestions for cooling a hothead:

1. *Control your tears.* The first fight after marriage usually leaves the bride in tears. This teaches the new husband, "Don't tell her her faults or she'll cry." Subcon-

sciously he may hold back communication to protect her.

God gave us tears. We are more complex emotionally than men and we often show our emotions with tears. Gentle tears may make a man feel protective and strong, but great heaving sobs only unnerve him, and make him want to get away, fast. In fact, a police officer told me he has never written a traffic ticket to a woman who sobbed hysterically when she was stopped.

Contrary to popular opinion, a man doesn't enjoy a knockdown, drag-out fight with his wife. Whether it's tears or shouting, he doesn't know how to cope with such emotion, but to protect his self-esteem, fights back.

When I'm mad at Charlie, I warn him ahead of time by telling him, "I'm going to get emotional. Wait a minute." Sometimes I run upstairs, cry, and feel sorry for myself. After I calm down and regain my composure, I return to carry on the conversation. I try not to sulk, nag, or refuse sex as punishment. I find that it's best to say what I have to say, and then forgive and forget.

Everyone at one time or another hurts or offends his mate. The next time your husband hurts you, instead of dwelling on what he did, think of how you will respond to his actions. What a lofty challenge! You can almost anticipate his thoughtlessness to practice your new, positive response.

2. *Plan the proper time and atmosphere.* Before you speak, think the problem through and put it into its proper perspective. An angry outburst can scar your hus-

band's emotions and create barriers between you. Stop and think before you blurt out what you might regret later on. Prepare to express your feelings without becoming emotional. Pray for discretion and love.

A cute cartoon shows an irritated husband asking his wife, "Must we try to save our marriage while I'm reading the sports page?" Your timing is so important. Don't meet your husband at the door with a club. Let him relax and give yourself time to judge his mood. If you save your problems until he is in a receptive mood, your chances of resolving them will be greatly increased. If you interrupt his favorite TV program, you can't expect him to be happy listening to what you have to say.

I have also found it's easier to resolve a conflict when my husband's blood sugar is high. The best time for me is shortly after dinner when his tummy is full and the children are in bed. But don't wait until after ten o'clock. Late at night problems loom larger and life seems darker. The difference between despair and hope is often a good night's sleep.

Set the atmosphere by telling him how important he is to you. Tell him you've tried to see the problem his way and you appreciate how he feels. Now you would also like for him to understand how you feel, regardless of what he chooses to do about it.

3. *Gently tell him what is in your heart*. The Bible advises us to speak the truth in love (21). Say exactly what's bothering you, but maintain your self-control. It was Shakespeare who wrote:

> Her voice was ever soft,
> Gentle, and low, an excellent thing in
>   woman.

Express your emotions in words, so that he'll know what's going on inside of you. Your main purpose should be to make your feelings understood, not to demand a change. When he understands how you feel, he may want to change whatever is bothering you.

Concentrate on your feelings, not on his faults. Instead of judging him by saying, "You never . . ." express your own feelings by saying, "I feel this way . . . ." If you accuse him, he will only attempt to justify his actions, even though he knows he is wrong; that's a law of life. If you raise your voice or become emotional, he will too. If you repeat yourself after you have told him your position, you're nagging. So say what you have to say in love and then thank him sincerely for listening. Give him time to react and think about what you have said. He may be hurt or he may explode, so allow for reaction time.

4. *Forgive and forget.* No matter what his reaction, your final step in dealing with anger is to forgive your husband and forget the incident. Forgiveness is essential for a great marriage. G. K. Chesterton said, "Forgiving means pardoning that which is unpardonable or it is no virtue at all." And just in case you feel your husband is entitled to only one mistake, remember that Jesus said to forgive seventy times seven (22). That's 490 times gals!

Some wives have terrible memories—they never forget

anything! Forgiving means forgetting. It means wiping the slate clean. The woman who doesn't forgive will probably suffer both physical fatigue and mental depression. It takes great emotional energy to carry a grudge. Our Lord taught us to pray, "Forgive us our sins; for we also forgive every one that is indebted to us . . ." (23). While on the cross He surely must have felt wronged and misunderstood, yet He prayed, "Father, forgive them . . ." (24). What a picture of forgiveness! What true love in action!

5. *Outroof him.* Statistics show there are more automobile accidents in the early-morning hours than at any other time of the day. The reason, studies conclude, is that husbands often leave home tense and angry, and take their frustrations out behind the wheel.

At a Total Woman coffee hour, Sue Borman, wife of astronaut Frank, verified this conclusion. An unusually high number of plane crashes occurred among the young pilots during Frank's early flight training. An investigation ensued, which revealed that often the crashes were directly related to the pilots' marital conflicts. Their problems at home overrode their ability to function properly. They simply could not cope with the inner turmoil and tensions, and took their emotions out on their machines.

Remember, your attitude not only sets the atmosphere in your home, but also determines your husband's attitude for the day. Out of your own resources of love and stability, you can choose to protect him from his own emotions. You can defer your anger by replacing it with understanding. In other words, you can choose to protect your husband!

During Bible days, apartment-type homes were built atop the city walls. Part of the roof extended beyond the walls to protect them from rain and sun. The word describing the overhang is *forbear*, which means "outroof," the same word used in the command to forbear one another in love (25). God tells us to outroof one another in love. Try it on your husband the next time he is upset and wants to pick a fight. You can protect him from his own emotions by outroofing him.

You can outroof him from fatigue. If he comes home miserable, maybe he is exhausted. You can protect him from too busy a social schedule by being sensitive to his preferences. He may not know how to get off the merry-go-round he is on. A loving wife canceled several Christmas parties on her hectic holiday calendar when she realized the stress within her husband. She reported that their season snuggling at home together was the jolliest Christmas ever.

By the way, the very next verse after "outroofing" states that you may have to run after peace (26). It's another way of saying, "Go the second mile." A Total Woman *chooses* to go the second mile. It really pays off.

12 *Blueprint for Blessings*

Jean and Tom hadn't communicated as husband and wife for months. They had considered divorce, but were hesitant because of Jimmy and Jody, their five-year-old twins. Jean called a friend one morning to say, "I've come to a conclusion about Tom—my silent partner. I'm not getting a divorce; I'm just going to ignore him around the house. I'll pour my life into the kids instead, so at least they'll turn out right."

But the question is, will they? Will Jimmy turn out right? Quite naturally Jimmy, as a little boy, identified with his dad. Although a composite of both parents, Jimmy's masculine qualities became dominant because of his father's influence.

Lately though, Tom wasn't available much to his family. He worked long hours and now his job required extensive travel. On weekends he always played golf with business associates. Jean had become possessive and overprotective of her children and Jimmy had begun to identify with his mother, who was available to meet his needs. Jean's decision to shun Tom and to raise the kids her way had thrown the household off balance. The family leadership was upside down.

It wasn't long before frictions developed between Jimmy and his dad, making communication difficult. Subconsciously, Jimmy began to lose respect for his father, and for his own sex as well. He began to feel unworthy. As the years go by, Jimmy may grow up weak in male attributes. In fact, he may not even know what they are. He is seldom with his father, and when he is, they never talk personally. He may identify with his mother and begin to develop certain feminine qualities on a subconscious level. Physically, he can appear quite masculine. Emotionally, however, because of his strong attachment to his mother, the door is open to homosexuality.

The chances of a normal marriage are slim for a man who grows up with a mother who calls the shots. If he does marry he usually finds a girl who controls him like his mother. The result of this ingrained pattern is a matriarchal society of dominant mothers and passive fathers.

Little girls also suffer in this kind of family. If Daddy is not available to cuddle his little girl, look at her drawings, and listen to her stories, she takes it personally. She thinks Daddy doesn't care. She may not reveal her feelings of rejection, but when she grows up she will transfer her resentment toward Daddy to all men, including her husband.

As women discuss this problem in class, it is interesting to see them gain insight into why they act the way they do. Afterward many choose to change by allowing the husband to lead the family. This permits the child to then see Dad in the masculine role and Mom in the feminine role. When the family is turned right side up, the child not only regains his respect for his parents, but is also able to accept himself.

Since it is the mother who determines whether her children will be burdens or blessings to the family and society, every child needs a Total Woman for a mother. I prefer the blessings route myself and have included my blueprint for these blessings.

Regrets or Rapport?

In their first six years of married life together, Sue and Larry had three bouncing baby girls. The enormity of his responsibility weighed heavily on Larry as he struggled to support the family. When he was home, Jackie, the youngest, was his pet. Larry showed her so much attention that even Sue became jealous of the way he catered to Jackie. Terry, the middle child, was clearly the tomboy of the clan, but that rubbed Larry the wrong way. He had wanted a boy to play ball with and to go to games together and had planned to name his boy Terry. He was so set on it that he named his girl Terry, but he unconsciously continued to blame her for her sex. Bonnie, the oldest, was mother's helper. She spent most of her time in the kitchen and seldom talked with her dad.

The straw that broke the camel's back, as well as Sue and Larry's, was when girl number four came along. She had three strikes against her even before she was born. She was little Miss Unwanted. Thus each of the girls, through no fault of her own was, to a certain extent, unaccepted by her parents.

Accepting your child is as important as accepting yourself and accepting your husband. Of course, you love your child, but are you harboring any regrets about who and what he is? Are you resentful, like Sue and Larry, because your child wasn't wanted, and his presence now hinders your activities? Are you jealous because your husband caters to your daughter instead of to you? Or does one child seem to grind on your nerves, constantly irritating and doing the wrong things at the wrong time? Are you trying to change him to fit into your mold?

When his parents constantly criticized his disheveled appearance and his poor grades, a teen-ager from Atlanta simply gave up and ran away. He thought he could never please his parents and the family would be happier if he weren't around. This example, of course, is repeated in homes throughout the country, simply because the runaway was never accepted at home.

One of the worst mistakes parents can make is to compare one child with another. He'll only hate the child he's being compared with, and resent you for it. He'll want to run away the first chance he has. If he isn't accepted for himself, he will grow up feeling inadequate, inferior, and insecure.

Mr. Johnson encouraged his son to play football, but the boy wanted to play the violin. The father never made the football team in college, and he wanted his son to make up for his failure. He continually compared his son with the other boys until finally the humiliated boy decided, "I don't fit in here. I'll leave. Somewhere, someone will accept me just as I am."

At times we force our children to do something because of social pressure or what people will think. Remember that people are to love, and things are to use. Yet it is so easy to reverse these rules. Don't use your child.

Rule number one: *Accept your child for what he is.*

I Love You

Love is the most important gift any parent can give. Your gifts will not buy your child's love; your child wants you! He wants to hear you say those words, "I love you." He needs constant physical expression of your love.

When he was a baby, remember how he loved to be held? He'll never outgrow that need to be touched. Fulfill that need; tell him you love him. Kiss him, hug him, and touch him every day. Perhaps the whole family needs to become more physically affectionate. You may feel self-conscious at first, but someone has to start. Hold your child on your lap if you're watching television, unless he's bigger than you! Hold hands whenever you can. As you pass him in the house, ruffle his hair and pat his arm. Give him a quick back rub when you tuck him in. And always be sure to kiss him good night.

A young woman who is an utter misfit in life told me her parents never wanted her. She lacks emotional security and confidence simply because her parents never expressed their love. "They never told me they loved me," she cried, "I know I'm no good to anybody."

If you and your husband express your love visibly and tell your child "I love you" every day, in his hour of need he may turn to you instead of to sex, crime, or drugs. But let him know that regardless of what he ever does, you'll always love him unconditionally.

A teen-ager confided to me recently, "I smoked pot for several months but then didn't touch the stuff for weeks. My parents found out about it and blew up. They couldn't forget it or forgive me. Finally it got so I couldn't stand it. I felt all alone with no one to turn to, but couldn't quite bring myself to suicide." Here was one child who needed his parents' unconditional love most of all when he had done wrong.

Rule number two: *Express love verbally and physically every day.*

Fun and Games

Three-year-old Susanne stayed in the kitchen while her mother cleaned up the breakfast dishes. She kept tugging at her mother's skirt, asking her to play dolls. Carolyn felt that being in the same room with her child was as good as playing. But this particular morning she realized the tugging said, "Love me, Mommy." Carolyn put her towel down, took the phone off the hook, and sat down on the floor. Susanne looked up with wide, starry eyes and exclaimed, "Mommy! Are we *playing?*" She knew the difference.

Let's face it. Life is hard at times and full of disappointments. But it's not all fun and games for your child, either. He lives in a sophisticated, amoral society with unique pressures on his front doorstep that children have never experienced before. He needs a road map through his preteen and teen-age years so that when he finally leaves the nest, he can fly confidently on his own. He looks to you to supply that road map. He is watching you—your standards, attitudes, and conduct, to see if he wants to adopt these for himself. As you play with your child and encourage him to take part in the family traditions, you are building his confidence. He'll be much more inclined to follow your way of life if you have been close throughout the years, playing and having fun together.

It doesn't necessarily take money to make life fun, just a little imagination and desire. For example, try making just one meal a week extraspecial. Make dinner memorable, not just a fuel stop. Celebrate. Stick a candle in the cake. Or stick it in the meat loaf. The important thing is to celebrate, even over silly little things. We women have special antennae for feeling. We can teach this to our families as we play together. Celebrate if the cat has kittens. Celebrate if Junior hits a home run. Celebrate if Daddy gets home early. Don't be too busy to be creative.

Last December my family had been shopping in the evening and each one was wrapping gifts in various rooms. I was lonely in the kitchen and asked them to bring all their presents into the kitchen and work in a private corner. They had a great time wrapping gifts while I cleaned up after dinner. I didn't feel resentful stuck in the kitchen, because my family was with me. We all had hilarious fun, clowning and running around the table. That night as I put Laura to bed, she grabbed me in a bear hug and said, "Oh, Mommy, I don't want to ever let go of you." And she is my aloof one!

Two weeks before each Halloween, Laura and Michelle and Daddy congregate in the kitchen and carve jack-o'-lanterns a little bit each night. The pumpkins grow "whiskers" by the time they're finished but the fellowship is marvelous. The kids have a ball, and I'm delighted to have their company. It's so cozy.

In February we work on valentines, and so on, around the year. Children love to take part in holiday traditions, birthdays, and anniversaries. Those hours spent working together on a project keep us unified as a family. We are building memories. And by the way, you'd be surprised at how deftly a daddy's big hands can paste doily lace!

I often wonder if a mother realizes how very important she is to her children? Are you your child's closest friend? Sure, he has his own companions, but they cannot take your place. He needs your friendship in a cheery home environment. He needs your personal undivided attention, which cannot be replaced with institutional care or day care.

Your child needs his father, too. Encourage your husband to play with the children, without nagging, of course! The average American father spends only a few minutes a week doing things his son wants him to do. Is it any wonder so many children won't listen to their fathers five or ten years later?

:

Aloise Steiner Buckley, mother of columnist William F. Buckley, Jr., and Senator James Buckley reminisced recently about the early years of the family that later became so prominent in the fields of politics, publishing, and business.

"When the children were little, it was marvelous," she recalled. "There was never a dull moment. We did everything together. We used to play games—Parcheesi and card games—with great competitive spirit.

"For years my husband wouldn't allow a radio in the house. That is the reason my children are well read. That, and my father's influence. I remember when I was small, he kept a big dictionary open on a stand and insisted that we look up any word we didn't understand."

During the Cuban missile crisis in 1961, President Kennedy was in the White House living quarters one evening when presidential aide Dave Powers came to deliver a message. As he entered the dimly-lit room, Dave heard the president speaking quietly and assumed that he was talking with a cabinet member. Peering around the corner, Dave was surprised to see the president sitting with his daughter Caroline on his lap, reading to her from a storybook. Even during a world crisis, this man could spend time with his children. Can we afford to do less?

Rule number three: *Play with your child.*

You are the Joneses!

A mother of four encouraged her youngest to sing, even though he had the worst voice in the family. The more he sang, the more she praised him. The boy gradually developed confidence in himself, and today is the leading soloist in the ninth grade.

We sometimes tend to criticize to make a child learn and obey. But constant criticism makes a child feel inferior and afraid. He thinks, "Mom doesn't love me. What's the use? If I can't please her, I might as well give up." This is the sentiment of many teen-agers today who have sold themselves out so cheaply.

Your child has an image of himself, just as you do. He determines his self-estimate from your words, actions, and attitudes toward him. He tends to become like the image he has of himself. If you keep telling him, "You're so stupid," he'll grow up thinking he is stupid. If you keep asking, "What is the matter with you?" he'll wonder what's the matter with him. But if you encourage him, he'll try harder. Instead of putting him down for what he didn't do, praise him for what he did do. It helps take out the sting. If you have been in the habit of criticizing this may take some practice, but it's well worth the effort.

Children need applause, figuratively and literally. Michelle detests green beans, so every time she eats her beans, we all applaud. I don't think she even tastes the beans now as they go down. She just revels in the applause!

Dr. Clyde Narramore tells the story of Mrs. Goodman, a third-grade teacher, who decided to compliment each of her thirty students every day. She said, "I think it's immoral to be around children all day and not to give them at least one compliment." Every day she checked off each name after complimenting the child. One day, little Johnny was such a terror that he failed to warrant any praise. It came time to leave and the teacher didn't want to ruin her record. Finally she told him, "You certainly were vital today!" And even that got a smile from Johnny!

Everyone loves encouragement. Most successful persons can point to a few people who, at the right time, encouraged them to do the seemingly impossible. Abraham Lincoln said, "Everything I ever did, I owe to my angel mother." He realized that his mother's belief in him had encouraged him to attain success.

It is almost impossible to overlove or give too much praise to your children. Just shower it on this week. Water that little green plant of yours with love and compliments. If he isn't watered regularly, he may dry up and wither inside. Make him feel secure, confident, and worthy.

The wife of a Texas judge told me, "My mother considered me a gift from God. All of us felt her love and faith in us. I always thought I could do anything I set out to do because Mother thought I could. She told me over and over, 'Never worry about keeping up with the Joneses—you *are* the Joneses!' "

What a heritage! Perhaps you did not have that confidence as a child, but you and I can give it to our children, not by tearing them down, but by building them up.

Rule number four: *Encourage your child.*

Serendipity Times

At the tender age of nine, Ann was sent to a girls' camp in North Carolina. Day by day her parents checked their mailbox at home. Finally after a week, a letter arrived which read:

Dear Mom and Dad,
My counselor said I should write home at least twice. This is once.

Love, Ann

Communication? At least the counselor thought so. The proper goal of all communication is not agreement between the parties, but understanding. Understanding is seeing things from the other person's point of view, knowing why he feels and acts the way he does. In order to understand your child, the communication gap must first be bridged by you. Often that involves more listening than talking. Your child feels that if you love him, you will be willing to listen to him. I find these suggestions help me in listening to my children.

1. *Be available*. My Laura needs me to listen when she needs to talk. If I am not available, or if I'm too busy, she may be gone when I'm ready to listen. One day after school, Laura brought home a girl friend. When I asked if her mother knew where she was, she told me, "It's all right, she doesn't care. I don't go home after school. There's no one there anyway." Her parents had given her

everything a child could ever ask in terms of material possessions, probably in an attempt to replace themselves. If this continues, I thought, she may one day turn to sex and drugs in order to get her parents' attention. What a price to pay!

2. *Be fun to talk to.* Every evening at dinner our family shares what Charles Shedd calls a "serendipity time." *Serendipity* means a pleasant, unexpected experience. Everyone in the family is encouraged to look positively at the day's events and share his one special highlight at dinner time. Sharing our serendipities is grass-roots drug prevention. The children feel accepted, loved, and turned on by the family fun, rather than through artificial means.

Charlie and I also share our life stories with the girls. It helps communication to be honest, so we tell our faults, failures, and funny times alike. One night I told Laura about my mom chasing me all over the neighborhood with a switch. She really identified with me and wanted to hear that story over and over! Laura is now old enough to recall her "childhood" and loves to tell her funny moments to her younger sister, Michelle.

3. *Be flexible and hear your child's side.* At a neighbor's house recently, I heard the father interrupt his son and cut off all communication by saying, "In this house, you'll think my way. That's final and we'll not discuss it anymore." Instead of trying to command your child to think your way, keep the lines of communication open so you'll know what he is thinking. If you have a close relationship with him, he will not be anxious to hurt you now or later.

But if you rant and rave, or spout false information, he will lose respect for you. He wants you to be secure in your position, and to be smarter than he is. If you are closed-minded, your child won't feel he can express his opinions, especially about sex and drugs, two of his greatest areas of pressure.

If he does share with you, don't run to your friend to tell it. If your child finds out, that's the end of intimate communication. If you love him, value your relationship enough to keep his confidence, regardless of how cute or juicy the comment.

4. *Be understanding.* One afternoon when I picked up Laura at school, she blurted out, "I just hate Susie." I tried to stay cool, and asked her why. She said, "I just hate her. She wouldn't let me play today at school." I started to tell her, "You shouldn't hate anybody," but swallowing my lecture, I asked her instead, "Do you hate Susie because she wouldn't let you play?" "I sure do," she said, and suddenly her face cleared and she was happy. Once she expressed her feelings and explained what was bothering her, she changed the subject. Her resentment was gone.

In responding to Laura's anger when she got in the car, I had simply reworded her comment and asked, "Do you hate Susie because she wouldn't let you play?" Psychologists use this procedure, called reflective counseling, to draw out the venom inside a person. A mother in one class hesitantly tried this procedure at home, not knowing quite how to go about it. Her daughter was practicing for a piano recital, and she kept whining nervously, "I just can't play that number." Instead of saying, "I know you're going to do fine," the mother asked, "Do you feel you might not do well in the recital, honey?" The girl cried, "Oh, Mom, you do understand. I want to be just like you when I grow up. We have the best family!" The mother never expected such a display of emotion, all from a remark that showed she understood. And the daughter didn't make one mistake in the recital!

Reflective counseling takes a little practice, but it's a great tool in communication. Reflect on what your child said and then repeat his thoughts back in slightly different words. This opens a little gate in his subconscious. He feels accepted and worthy, and is then willing to volunteer a little more. Help release his anger and fears now, so he won't have repressed hostilities and depression later in life.

Rule number five: *Talk with your child.*

Boundary Disputes

Recently over lunch I talked with a young woman who was experiencing deep emotional problems. She recalled how as a child she watched her parents' reactions when she disobeyed. When they failed to discipline her, she thought they were afraid of her. One day when she was thirteen she threw such a tantrum that her mother gave in and said, "Oh, go ahead. I don't care what you do." That was the turning point in her young life. She thought her mother really didn't care because she had failed to discipline her. At the moment of her mother's abdication,

:

the girl thought, "You fool!" From that day on she was on her own. She went from man to man looking for love. Today, this miserable wife finds self-control extremely difficult.

In another case, a teen-ager was late one night for curfew, but her mother was tired and overlooked the misdemeanor. The next morning the phone rang at half-past eight. The teen-ager told her mother, "It's Bill. We want to go shopping today; but first, what's my punishment for coming in late last night?" She felt guilty and didn't want to carry the burden of guilt. She wanted it resolved and had actually asked for discipline.

As a child, Charles Manson, the convicted murderer, was continually pampered and usually got his own way. Because he was never disciplined, he never learned self-control. Years later the consequences bore bitter fruit. Studies of divergent youth show that a child who grows up without boundaries often cannot control himself in a sensible, consistent manner as an adult. He feels unloved, frustrated, and rejected.

Discipline is child training. People sometimes equate "discipline" with spanking, but discipline is positive training—what you do *for* a child, not just what you do *to* him. Discipline consists of two basic steps: setting limits in love, and correcting in love when these limits are broken. A parent who is fearful to limit, afraid to forbid, and unwilling to train, sends his child into the tangle-wood of life without a knowledge of the trails.

1. *Set limits in love.* Dave, a friend's fourteen-year-old, told his parents, "But Dad, everybody smokes grass."

Secretly, Dave was afraid and wanted his folks to say, "No, you cannot use drugs of any kind." However, instead of telling him no, they said, "It's up to you. But if you do, we won't like it." Dave wasn't strong enough to resist without a stronger stand by his parents, and now two years later, he is a regular user of heroin.

Be willing to set standards for your child. Let him know what is expected of him. He will only feel secure when he knows the limits of what he can and cannot do. More than one delinquent has said, "No one cared enough to tell me what to do."

True love protects a child from harm by keeping him from playing with fire. It is love that limits—for love's sake. It has been said that if God had wanted parents to be permissive, He would have given us the Ten Suggestions instead of the Ten Commandments! It is a child's nature to try to test his parents' limits, but as long as these limits hold firm, he feels safe.

Be firm and positive; offer your children constructive alternatives. Distraction is not only a great tool for little ones, but it also works wonders for big brother. If you condemn your child's friends, he will be forced to defend them. Offer new friends, new activities, and new interests. It is always easier to take away a cracker when you offer a cookie in its place.

Don't despair if your family doesn't agree on every issue. To expect total accord is unrealistic. Children have ideas of their own which may be contrary to yours. When a father refused to allow his daughter to go to a certain party, he said, "Whether you agree with me or not, I'll

:

always love you, because I am your father. Nothing can change that. In fact, it's because I love you that you're not going to that party." He did not ask her to change her convictions, but only to forego her actions. The daughter was heartbroken and angry with her father at the time. He told her he realized how upset she was, but he had to follow *his* convictions. Years later, the daughter told her dad how she remembered that occasion and was secretly thankful for his strong stand.

You may never hear your children admit you were right, but nevertheless you must do for them what you know is right. Parenthood is not a popularity contest.

As your child is growing up, give him responsibility as fast as he can handle it. But don't forget that he is only a child and cannot handle his job as you would. He needs years of training and supervision to learn, and that's why you are needed at home. Patiently help him until he can accept some responsibility and then give him some more. Remember that we are not machines and neither is your child. Life is a series of adjustments, so be flexible and don't be too rigid to change if change is necessary.

2. *Correct him in love.* When your child oversteps the limits you have set for him, it is your responsibility to correct him in love. Dr. James Dobson, author of *Dare to Discipline* writes, "When he flops his hairy little toe across the line you've drawn, that's the time to give it to him."

Children are naturally disobedient, starting at about age fifteen months and lasting through adolescence. An obedient child is made, therefore, not born. The Bible, the original "how to do it" Book, directs parents to discipline their children in love. According to the Proverbs, spanking is still in. "Foolishness is bound in the heart of a child; but the rod of correction shall drive it far from him" (27). "Chasten thy son while there is hope, and let not thy soul spare for his crying" (28). "Withhold not correction from the child: for if thou beatest him with the rod, he shall not die" (29). I guess God knew those heartbreaking moans would get to us. And if you think you love your child too much to spank him, the Bible also declares, "He who spares the rod hates his son, but he who loves him is diligent to discipline him" (30).

If your child challenges your authority, he is testing you to see if you really mean what you say. Before you can guide him, you must first earn the right to do it. When Laura deliberately disobeys, I tell her, "I love you too much to allow you to act that way." Spanking clears the air. I always love and hug her afterward and the rapport is reestablished. She feels secure in knowing I am secure in my position. When I assure her I love her regardless of her behavior, I don't feel guilty and she isn't bitter.

I remember seeing a cartoon years ago showing the smoldering ruins of a house destroyed by fire. The father was looking forlornly at the heap of rubble as the mother told her little daughter, "Mommy and Daddy are not mad at you, Marilyn. Mommy and Daddy are mad at the naughty thing you've done."

The context of the cartoon was humorous, but the principle was true. The parents loved their daughter, but were mad at her actions. Always distinguish that difference and try not to spank your child when you are furiously angry. If you have fire in your eyes, you'll only scare him and he will not believe you have his best interest at heart.

When a close friend spanked his three-year-old for hitting the baby, he did it in a loving way. Afterward the child hugged him and said, "Thank you for saying no, Daddy!" Your goal in discipline should be to train up self-disciplined, self-controlled children. The Bible says, "Train up a child in the way he should go: and when he is old, he will not depart from it" (31). What a wonderful promise!

Don't be discouraged if you feel it's too late for you and your children. It's not! Another one of my favorite promises from the Bible is, "I will restore to you the years that the locust hath eaten . . ." (32). As I prepared this material I wished I could have started over with my children. Maybe you will, too, but God can *restore* those years.

Rule number six: *Discipline your child in love.*

Don't Keep the Faith

A reporter asked Rose Kennedy if she had but one thing to leave her children, what would it be? She answered, "Certainly it wouldn't be money and estate, or any other material thing, nor even success, could I guarantee it. Faith! It's the most important, the one legacy I would choose to pass on. When we have faith we are happy, because God is directing our lives, our work and our play. You know," she paused, only a flicker, "we need a sense of direction, a purpose to our life. Faith gives us confidence."

Every child has a natural hunger for God. Little Billy, looking in the closet and under the bed, told his mother he was looking for God. Children of all ages are searching for Him. Often they don't see anyone who has a relevant relationship with God so they begin looking in the wrong direction.

Don't keep the faith, gals; pass it on. To help your child find God, I suggest a few simple but most effective activities.

1. *Read the Bible to your children every day.* In Old Testament times, God instructed Israel to tell its children, "You shall love the LORD your God with all your heart, and with all your soul, and with all your might. . . . and you shall teach [these words] diligently to your children . . . in your house . . . when you walk . . . when you lie down, and when you rise" (33).

While driving through the North Carolina mountains a few summers ago, Laura said she was too busy working a puzzle in the backseat to see the gorgeous view opening before us. She couldn't see the peaks for the puzzle.

When she finally looked up, she saw a road sign which read, CURVY ROAD AHEAD. I told her God also puts up signs to show us we can avoid troubles up ahead. Sometimes He says, "Stop! Danger ahead," and at other times He says, "Yield." He doesn't want us spending wasted years because of an unfortunate detour, and has left us the Bible as our road map.

The Bible has much to say about our lives today, as well as what's going to happen in the near and distant future. Anyone can be informed and confident if he only makes the effort to read that Book. Our children are especially sensitive to the uncertainties of the times, and need the stability of everlasting truth.

In the mornings before sunrise, I love to go downstairs to read quietly by myself. The quietness of that time of solitude helps prepare me for whatever might come that day.

One particular morning, I picked up the Bible and became so engrossed that I didn't see my little girl standing beside me. After a bit, Laura said, "Mom, tell me what you're reading." As we talked Laura grasped the meaning. We talked heart to heart, and soul to soul. By then the rest of the family had awakened and was asking for breakfast. As we went into the kitchen, Laura hugged me and crooned, "Mama, dear, sweet Mama, I love you."

Tender expressions like that are so rare for my little girl. I believe in those moments of sharing she had taken in spiritual nourishment and her little soul was overflowing with love. I find that those occasional early-morning hours together are the only quiet times during the day when we can delve into that Book of Love.

2. *Provide spiritual resources.* Give your child good books on drugs, sex, and current events, all with a spiritual emphasis. Books can tell your child what you are unable to think or say. He has access to all the dirty and perverted literature he wants. Help him by making good books readily and equally available.

Music is also a great influence in helping your child to love God. A little child memorizes so easily and stores the material in his computer for life. If you teach him spiritual songs, when he is grown one of those songs may bring him back to God. Sacred records are a must. Around our house, the girls' favorites, and ours, are those by Anita Bryant.

Take time to explain the lyrics from familiar hymns like, "incarnate, ascribed, and pavilioned." For fifteen years, I thought "prostrate" was a gland. The words of the old hymns of the faith are lovely if you know what they mean, but how can a child enjoy singing in a language he never learned? A teen-ager from Brooklyn heard for the first time, "We shall come rejoicing, bringing in the sheaves." He went home at noon and said, "Guess what we sang? 'We shall come from Joisey, bringing in the sheets!'"

When my Laura was very little, she heard me singing, "Jesus took my burdens all away." She seemed distressed as I sang that song. When she was old enough, she asked me why Jesus took the birdies all away!

So many teen-agers today are bitter toward their parents. The reason many give for this hostility is their parents' hypocrisy and inconsistency. The parents do not practice their preaching. Spiritual leadership in the home cannot start with the children. The parents must set the example through their own lives and by providing sacred music, books, and records in their children's pliable and formative years. Unless they see faith in action in their parents' lives, they will reject the faith of their fathers.

3. *Pray with the family.* I asked a banker recently, "What are the most vivid memories of your father?" He thought for a moment and then said, "Two things: one, I remember him rolling on the floor with me, laughing and playing. The other that I'll always remember is peeking in my parents' room early one morning and seeing my father on his knees, praying."

Your child needs a hot line to heaven, just like you do. A teen-age girl confided, "I wish my parents would pray with me. Then I'd know they *really* care." When a problem comes up, or a friend asks me to pray for her, I ask my little girl to pray with me. Laura is growing up praying over problems she doesn't always understand, but she knows we are taking the problems to the One who does. She is learning to follow the scriptural principle of bearing one another's burdens.

Suzannah Wesley had nineteen children. She took care of their personal needs and gave each of them all their formal education. Besides all that, she prayed for and with each one individually every day. When she pulled her apron over her head in the midst of the bedlam, the children knew they must be quiet because Mother was talking to God on their behalf. She produced two mighty men of God, Charles and John Wesley. So if you need a challenge, remember Suzannah!

Rule number seven: *Encourage spiritual growth in your children.*

13 Power Source

One day recently, Laura came home from school loaded with three books, a doll, and her lunch box. Anxious to play, she dropped them all on the kitchen floor. I heard the crunch of the lunch box and took out the Thermos bottle. It looked fine on the outside, but inside the glass was shattered in a million little pieces. Looking at that lining, I thought, "Little Thermos bottle, I identify with you. How many times I've felt just like you look—shattered!"

When you feel like Humpty Dumpty, who had a great fall, who puts you back together again? When your husband cuts you down, who gives you the power to keep on loving? When you want to pop him one for spoiling your plans, who gives you self-control? Is it possible to maintain a relaxed mental attitude when pressures seem overwhelming? Where are you going, anyway? And why?

So far in this book, we've taken your old house, the

fragmented you, and painted the outside. We've planted some new shrubs and repaired a few loose shutters. Inside, we've dusted under the sofa and done some redecorating. All we need now is the power. Without a power source for heat, for light, for life, your shell is nothing more than a glorified outhouse.

Ten years ago I "plugged in" to the world's greatest power source. I established contact with my Creator, the Source and Essence of love—perfect love. He gave me life, with a capital L. He turned on all the lights, brighter than I had ever seen. And He put all my pieces together again.

My Search

From my earliest recollection of my childhood, I recall my love for God. I believed in Him with all my heart, but somehow I couldn't seem to make contact. I never doubted He existed, but my prayers seemed to bounce off the ceiling. I was frustrated over my one-way love affair. I pleaded with Him, but He never seemed to respond.

My father's death when I was fourteen completely broke my heart. After the funeral, I remember taking a long walk through a cornfield behind my house. I sobbed and prayed. No answer. Dad was gone and God wouldn't answer. "God, if you're out there," I shouted, "why don't you let me know it?" But there was still no answer. My prayers bounced again.

In the years that followed, I began to search for Him in stained-glass windows. I called ministers and priests at random and asked for an appointment to discuss my search. Some were too busy, they said. Others never bothered to return my call. One minister said he, too, was looking, and to call if I ever found it. Religion left me cold.

I had always tried to be a "good little girl." On Saturdays I baked cookies and delivered them to sick people's doorsteps anonymously. I took presents on holidays to the less fortunate across town. I wanted to make the world a better place. My search continued.

At Ohio State University, I studied philosophy. I read the various philosophers until I collapsed each night. I found myself confused, however, as I tried to take the best from each. So many claimed to be "truth," yet they contradicted each other. Some of these were real humdingers. They seemed good enough to live by, but not good enough to die by.

My involvement with people was the most fun, and brought me the most happiness. College life was active with academic honors and campus and state beauty contest awards. Even a trip to Europe didn't satisfy. Under it all, there was that one problem. My song was the pop song, "Laughing on the Outside, Crying on the Inside." And I didn't even know why I was crying!

I felt empty inside. I felt guilty. I longed for something more. I was afraid to be alone with my thoughts. Turning the radio on full blast helped drown out my searching questions. Why am I here? Where am I going? What's it all about, Marabel? As I walked to class each morning I sang to keep up my courage. My favorite was, "Let a Smile Be Your Umbrella." No one ever suspected otherwise. I played the role well.

When I first realized the importance of money, I was sure I had found the real secret to life. Dollars could buy happiness. The more dollars, the greater the options, the greater the joy. In the tenth grade, I remember shopping for a sweater and then I saw it—the most luscious, furry, beige sweater I'd ever seen. That sweater had to be mine. I wanted it more than anything in the world. I stood at the department store window every day on my way home and pictured it on me.

Money was hard to come by then, but I finally saved enough to buy it. I still remember how anxious I was during classes that day and how I rushed downtown after school. Oh, it was such a big deal. I remember every detail, even the closet-like fitting room with pins on the floor, where I slipped it on and the miracle took place. That sweater made me look ethereal.

That night, however, when I tried it on again at home, that terrible lonely feeling swept over me. "So! I've got the sweater," I thought, "but I still feel empty inside." It left a permanent impression. Things didn't satisfy. That sweater was my goal of the moment. "If only it were mine," I had thought, "I'd be satisfied." But I wasn't. To have it turn to ashes in my mouth was so unexpected. It really rocked me.

What *was* the answer? I asked myself that question repeatedly while walking to work on clear summer mornings. I watched the yellow butterflies darting over the waving wheat fields and knew that the God who created all this must have something more for me. I said aloud, "If only I could really see; if I could just pull the blinders off my eyes and see life as it really is." I looked at my hands and thought about the blood coursing through those veins. I was awed at the magnitude of the human body. I thought, "*I'm* in this body. The real me lives in here. But, who am I actually? Who am I?"

I felt there must be something more, a dimension of life that I just could not perceive, but I knew by this time that it had to come from a greater source than myself.

Transformed, not Reformed

My search finally led me to truth—ageless truth, satisfying and relevant. A friend told me that God loved me and had a wonderful plan for my life. I knew that God is love and I could quote John 3:16 even as a child: "For God so loved the world, that he gave his only begotten Son, that whosoever believeth in him should not perish, but have everlasting life."

God's love, for me! And Jesus said He came to give us abundant life (34). That sounded good to me. But how did I plug into this God of the universe?

Thousands of years ago, the Jewish prophet Isaiah said, "Your iniquities have separated between you and your

God . . ." (35). Thousands of years ago, or yesterday, or today? Were my iniquities, my sins, keeping me from God and His power? I wasn't a bad kid and I wanted to see what qualified as "sin." I came across a list in the Bible that astounded me. They weren't gross sins, but the garden variety—worry, unbelief, gossiping, pride.

Wow, I hit the jackpot. That was me. I was separated and unplugged. I had spent twenty-three lonely years separated from God. At times it was nearly unbearable to experience that devastating loneliness, that emptiness.

And then there was more bad news. "The penalty for sin," my friend said, "is death—spiritual death—according to Romans 6:23."

"Oh, no, I'm a goner," I remember thinking. "I'm a sinner for sure, and the sentence has been pronounced." I looked at my dear friend and she must have seen my total despair.

She said, "But, there's good news, too, right there in the same verse '. . . but the gift of God is eternal life through Jesus Christ our Lord'" (36). I saw that Marabel couldn't bridge the chasm back to God, so God reached down to Marabel. That was good news. That was great news! My friend then showed me a verse in the Bible which seemed to contradict all my attempts to reach God. It read, "For by grace are ye saved through faith; and that not of yourselves: it is the gift of God: Not of works . . ." (37).

I saw how, long ago, God stepped out of eternity and stepped into time. He came so that man could come out from wherever he was hiding and be free. The world had been expecting Him ever since the prophets had described the coming Messiah.

I eagerly read His writings. His life was one of total unselfishness. He seemed to spend so much of His life healing broken bodies and broken hearts. His personal claims were unique. He claimed, for example, to be the sole way any man could reach God the Father. He even spoke of His impending death, explaining that He came to be our Passover Lamb, my Passover Lamb.

Because He died, I could live. He promised me life. My friend showed me Revelation 3:20, where Jesus stood knocking at a symbolic door of my heart: "Behold, I stand at the door, and knock: if any man hear my voice, and open the door, I will come in to him, and will sup with him, and he with me."

I could hardly wait to ask Him into my life, once I realized the importance of this step. I had always believed in God and in Jesus, His Son. I believed He had died years ago as the Saviour of man. But now He became my Saviour.

I prayed to God silently, "Dear God, I've been looking for You for so long. Thank You for finding me. I believe that Jesus died—for me, as my Saviour. I invite Him into my life right now. Thank You very much. Amen."

I looked up at my friend and began to weep with joy. I realized that my search was over; my lifelong, agonizing search. I felt so clean, so complete. I was plugged in, at last! Not reformed, but transformed—hooked up to the true power source—the Light of the world. The lights came on and they've never gone out.

Forever Family

Since that all-important day, I've experienced the most wonderful benefits of the abundant life, which He promised to give.

First of all, I have peace—inner peace from God Himself, the Prince of Peace. Jesus said, ". . . my peace I give unto you . . ." (38). I am His very own child, spiritually born into the forever family!

Secondly, I have pardon. Jesus paid the penalty for my sins, all I ever did or ever will do wrong. Jesus promised, "Ye shall know the truth, and the truth shall make you free" (39). By receiving Him, I am acquitted, set free, made a liberated woman.

Thirdly, I have a purpose in life. For so many years, I wondered, "Who am I? Where am I going?" My Jesus is the Way—the Way out—the Way through. He is my reason for living.

Lastly, I have power. His Power. He is not dead. He arose from the dead. He's alive. He said that His same resurrection power can be mine. I have the power to live the abundant life—power to love—power to transform my natural love for my husband and children into a super love, a divine love, flowing out of me.

You, too, can plug into this power Source. Your life can have peace, pardon, purpose, and power. Because God is love, contact with Him means abundant life for you, and a super love for others. The Bible promises that you will become a new person inside and a new life will begin.

To invite Him into your life, simply open the door. Talk to Him. The following is a suggested prayer which many in the classes have used successfully.

Dear Jesus, I need You. I open the door of my life and receive You as my Saviour. Thank You for forgiving my sins. Make me the kind of person You want me to be. Thank You for coming in as You promised You would.

Please, don't be satisfied with a new paint job and some redecoration. Plug yourself into the One, the only One, who can give you life. Pascal said, "There is a god-shaped vacuum in the heart of every man, which cannot be satisfied by any created thing, but only by God, the Creator . . . ." God is waiting and wanting to fill your vacuum, to make you complete. Total. Right now you can become a Total Woman.

Assignment: Building Bridges

To Your Husband

1. When you have good rapport with your husband this week, ask him to write out your three main strengths and weaknesses. Thank him for his helpful list. Don't be defensive as you read it.
2. Celebrate something special tonight. Make dinner time a time of fun and sharing. Plan to have a serendipity time for him and the children.

To Your Children

1. Put into practice today with each child the blueprint for blessings:
   a. Accept him
   b. Love and touch him
   c. Play with him
   d. Encourage him
   e. Talk with him
   f. Discipline him in love
   g. Encourage spiritual growth
2. List the characteristics that you would like to develop in your children. Begin to compliment these traits as you see them appear.

To Your God

1. Read the third chapter of Saint John in a modern translation of the Bible. Buy a copy if you don't have one.

2. Jesus has bridged the gap between you and God. This free gift of life is now yours for the asking.

14 Conclusion

Dear Help!

Dear Marabel,

I enjoyed seeing you again at our high-school class reunion. Sorry I appeared so upset, but I am in such a frazzled state because I am involved in so much outside my home. I know my mistakes. I have spread myself too thin. It is very difficult to have the house shipshape, all the clothes clean and put away, and still have time with my children and husband, when I am responsible for so many other things. I sit at the typewriter or on the phone three or four days each week.

I feel guilty. I feel like my children have the right to my time and attention, but how today or tomorrow do I resolve this problem? I have thought of resigning from the church and club offices, but would feel like a quitter.

My husband and I hope to have another baby shortly. I will absolutely say no to *any* outside activities then. But what do I do about tomorrow? I have always been interested, active, and involved, but my timing is off. Our children are so young (four years and twenty-two months). I *know* I should be home. All of this causes me to be so critical of myself. Why am I not more organized? Why don't I spend more time with the children? I am tired, just plain tired. My first and most important responsibility is to my family, I know this. I believe it.

But I have always had such a sense of responsibility, a sense of seeing things through to completion. I keep saying these outside activities won't last forever. Meanwhile, I am in a constant state of contradiction. What would a Total Woman do?

Help!

Dear Help!

It is impossible to explain Total Woman in a ten-minute conversation, or in a four-week course, or in a how-to-do-it book. Total Woman is a way of life, a new attitude about yourself, your husband, and your children.

Total Woman starts with the premise that every woman can be made whole. Even with the complex facets to her personality and the many roles to play, no woman need go through life fragmented.

A Total Woman is not just a good housekeeper; she is a warm, loving homemaker. She is not merely a submissive sex partner; she is a sizzling lover. She is not just a nanny to her children; she is a woman who inspires them to reach out and up.

A Total Woman is a person in her own right. She has a sense of personal security and self-respect. She is not afraid to be herself. Others may challenge her standards, but she knows who she is and where she is going.

She has the gift of discovering what is worthwhile in another person. She dares her husband to rise higher than he ever dreamed. She makes marriage enjoyable instead of an endurance contest. She has a natural love affair with life and brings life to others.

You can be that Total Woman, with your priorities in order and your responsibilities in perspective. First of all, remember that you are a *person* responsible to God, your power Source. Until you become the kind of woman He wants you to be, you will not be able to fully give yourself to others, for you have little to give. Fill your cup vertically before you attempt to give to others horizontally.

Your second priority is to your husband, your *partner*. Too many husbands get lost in the shuffle after Junior arrives, or are replaced by their wives' other activities. Your husband needs to know he's tops on your list.

Your next priority is as a *parent* to your children. Good mothers are not born; they are made by women who want to be good mothers. In those early years, your children need their mom at home. Their future development is far more important than your sorority ball.

Only after you have met your spiritual needs, the needs of your husband and your children, should you think of your *profession* or the *public*. Civic clubs, parties, and social projects, yes, but only after order is restored at home.

I wish you well.

Marabel

Survival Kit

During a Total Woman class, one young woman arrived late and dramatically threw her hand across her forehead. Sighing, she implored, "Can this marriage be saved?" She was joking, but her question might have been rephrased, "Will love survive marriage?" I suggest that it can, with the help of your survival kit. As you begin your homework, you should see some changes in your life. I'd like to offer three final suggestions as you start:

1. *Don't dwell on your past mistakes.* If the water is already over the dam, there's no way to change it now. Why worry over something you cannot change or control? I overheard a woman in class mutter under her breath, "I've been doing so many things wrong for so many years, it's a wonder that I'm still married." I've heard some other women cry over their past, but that's good too, for tears are healing. When you see your mistake it does cause pain. But when you gain insight into why you are the way you are, you can then choose to change. See your mistakes and admit them, but don't dwell on them.

2. *Don't be discouraged when you slip back into old bad habits.* A close friend told me how she had stood at her kitchen sink one night with a clenched fist, fuming over something her husband had said. She thought to herself, "I don't care what that old course says, I'm really going to let him have it." But then she remembered that her explosion method was usually ineffective anyway, so

there over the sink she regained control. She changed her attitude and that worked!

Even if you blow it occasionally gals, get up and try it again. Don't be too hard on yourself. A Total Woman is also human.

3. *Concentrate on your own potential.* Don't forget that your husband hand picked you from all the other girls. To him, you are something special, and have (or had) something that appeals to him. Develop that unique potential. The sky is the limit in your relationship with him. You have everything to gain and very little to lose by trying.

World Champions

Several months ago I was the guest on a local television talk show. After some discussion the emcee opened the telephones for reactions from the residents. Most of the calls came from housewives, but one man called in to say:

> I am disgusted that Mrs. Morgan didn't have problems a little bit sooner so that I could have solved my marital problems and been married today. Everything she said on the program is exactly what took place in my marriage. I was just unable to relate to my wife or get the point across that she was nagging and not letting me be somewhat independent, which is my nature. Had she been able to take this course, I think that today I would be happily married and be able to share the joys of not only my wife, but my child.

After each Total Woman class, we ask for reactions to the course from both the girls and their husbands. One sad-looking woman handed me her note. As I read it, I thought that she might have been married to that gentleman who had called in. "If I had taken a course like this seventeen years ago," it read, "I am sure my husband wouldn't have left me. Because of it I had to bring up my children by myself. All these years I was sure I had done the right thing, but now I see where I was wrong. Now my goal is to give my daughter the information she will need to have a happy life when she gets married."

Other comments are more encouraging and often humorous. One woman wrote, "My husband said, 'I don't know what I have done to deserve all this!' My children said, 'Mommy is happy since she started her class!' We have been married twenty-three years and really needed a boost for the next forty-three!"

One husband told his wife after the sex assignment, "You're too much! You're crazy. I never know what you're going to do next. I love you. What? Another costume?" The wife added a note: "P.S. Marabel, our sex life is 100 percent better!"

Another husband said, "To me, T.W. means 'Terrific Wife.' If things get any better I can't take it. I feel like I've found my wife again after the seven-year itch. I wish this course was compulsory for marriage."

It was Balzac who wrote that a woman must be a genius to create a good husband. You can be that genius as a Total Woman. Many women have.

Attending one of the first classes in Miami were wives of the Miami Dolphin football players. Mrs. Bob Griese, Mrs. Howard Twilley, Mrs. Norm Evans, Mrs. Karl Noonan, Mrs. Tim Foley, Mrs. Jesse Powell, Mrs. Mike Kolen, Mrs. Bob Heinz, Mrs. Vern Den Herder, Mrs. Jack Clancy, and Mrs. John Richardson listened well and really tackled their assignments that night. They sought to put their husbands first and bring out the very best in them.

By the way, it is interesting to note that their team won every game that next season and became the world champions! It was the first undefeated season in the history of professional football, including play-off games and the Super Bowl.

Gals, I wouldn't dream of taking credit for the Super Bowl, nor can I promise *you* perfect success. But I can assure you of one thing—once the inside of your house is decorated; once the outside of your house is painted; once your power source is the Light of the world, you will find yourself in a new and exciting dimension—one where you, too, can become a super wife and a Total Woman.

The Beginning

Scripture References

1   James 1:2   PHILLIPS
2   Proverbs 16:3   KJV
3   John 8:32   KJV
4   Matthew 19:19   KJV
5   Psalms 139:14   KJV
6   Ephesians 5:22   LB
7   Acts 20:35   KJV
8   Genesis 2:23   KJV
9   Genesis 1:28   LB
10 Genesis 1:31   KJV
11 Verse 5   KJV
12 Romans 5:12   KJV
13 1 Corinthians 7:5   PHILLIPS
14 Proverbs 5:19   KJV
15 Hebrews 13:4   KJV
16 Proverbs 5:19
17 Ephesians 4:26   KJV
18 Proverbs 15:1   KJV
19 Ephesians 4:26   KJV
20 see Hebrews 12:15   KJV

21 see Ephesians 4:15   KJV
22 see Matthew 18:22   KJV
23 Luke 11:4   KJV
24 Luke 23:34   KJV
25 see Ephesians 4:2   KJV
26 see Ephesians 4:3   KJV
27 Proverbs 22:15   KJV
28 Proverbs 19:18   KJV
29 Proverbs 23:13   KJV
30 Proverbs 13:24   RSV
31 Proverbs 22:6   KJV
32 Joel 2:25   KJV
33 Deuteronomy 6:5, 7   RSV
34 see John 10:10   KJV
35 Isaiah 59:2   KJV
36 Romans 6:23   KJV
37 Ephesians 2:8, 9   KJV
38 John 14:27   KJV
39 John 8:32   KJV

Total Woman, Inc.
Bibliography

Carnegie, Dale. *How to Win Friends & Influence People.* Tadworth, Surrey: World's Work Ltd. (Windmill Press), 1938.

Dobson, James. *Dare to Discipline.* Wheaton, Illinois: Tyndale House Publishers, 1972.

Glasser, William. *Reality Therapy.* New York: Harper & Row, Publishers, 1965.

Haggai, John E. *How to Win Over Worry and Fear.* Grand Rapids: Zondervan Publishing House, 1967.

LaHaye, Tim. *How to be Happy Though Married.* Wheaton, Illinois: Tyndale House Publishers.

Miles, Herbert J. *Sexual Happiness in Marriage.* Grand Rapids: Zondervan Publishing House, 1967.

Missildine, W. Hugh. *Your Inner Child of the Past.* New York: Simon & Schuster, Inc., 1963.

Osborne, Cecil. *The Art of Understanding Your Mate.* Grand Rapids: Zondervan Publishing House.

Robinson, Marie N. *The Power of Sexual Surrender.* Garden City, New York: Doubleday & Company, Inc., 1959.

Smith, Hannah W. *The Christian's Secret of Happy Life.* Old Tappan, New Jersey: Fleming H. Revell Company, 1968.

Smith, Kenneth G. *Learning to Be a Woman,* Downers Grove, Illinois: Inter-Varsity Press, 1970.

Tournier, Paul. *Marriage Difficulties.* London: S.C.M. Press, 1967.